"Dr. Lavender is a pastor committed to  on the history of preaching and its failur is helpful and up to date, and the helpfi poor preparation and training prove to be very valuable. The thought-provoking questions asked in the book will need an answer, and I believe that Dr. Lavender's comments will benefit any preacher. I am happy to recommend this book to anyone interested in the faithful communication of God's Word."

—*Daniel J. Griffin Sr., international pastor and director of international training, Sanctuary Outpost*

"*Enduring Truth* is a powerful and passionate call for African Americans to re-institute sound theological preaching to the pulpit. Christ is exalted at the turn of every page and Lavender's steadfastness to the Bible's authority will keep the reader grounded in the truth and thesis of the work. The discussion questions are good for personal reflection and small group discussions. I would recommend *Enduring Truth* for any pastor seeking personal growth or a resource for pastoral training programs. In addition, it's a great book for faculty teaching a preaching course."

—*Kevin Jones, assistant professor of teacher education, Boyce College*

"Dr. Aaron Lavender addresses the textual accuracy and the relevance of biblical preaching. He expounds on elements of racial segregation: historical, social, educational, and religious. Dr. Lavender explains the awareness of discrimination and the struggle with African Americans having a distorted view of God's Word, and answers the age-old question, 'What is truth?' Every serious student of the Word would benefit from reading this book."

—*Allen R. McFarland, senior pastor, Calvary Evangelical Baptist Church*

"This book is a candid, succinct, and needed treatise on why so many African American pulpits are under-serving their congregants. As a teacher of church history, I heartily endorse this book. The author fearlessly names people and ministries that have contributed to the abuse and misapplication of God's Word, even today. And while the emphasis is on African American pulpits, the need to restore sound theology is universal. It is a must read!"

—*LeRoy Randolph Jr., president emeritus and director of institutional advancement, Carver Baptist Bible College, Institute, & Theological Seminary*

ENDURING TRUTH

RESTORING SOUND THEOLOGY & RELEVANCE
TO AFRICAN AMERICAN PREACHING

AARON E. LAVENDER

Nashville, Tennessee

DEDICATION

*This book is dedicated to my lovely,
devoted, and supportive wife, Ledora.*

Contents

Acknowledgments

HEARTFELT thanks to pastoral staff colleagues Reverend Charles Bryant Sr. and Reverend Brett Campbell Sr. Thanks, my brothers, for your input and insightful suggestions.

I thank my Lord and Savior, Jesus Christ, "who has enabled me, in that He counted me faithful, putting me into the ministry" (1 Tim 1:12 HCSB).

Introduction

E VER since the catastrophic events in the garden of Eden, God's Word has been distorted. God explicitly forbade Adam from eating fruit from the tree of the knowledge of good and evil, telling him, "But of the tree of the knowledge of good and evil, thou shalt not eat of it: for in the day that thou eatest thereof thou shalt surely die" (Gen 2:17). God's Word to Adam was precise and well-defined. Adam presumably, in turn, was responsible for communicating God's Word to Eve in the same manner it had been communicated to him—word for word without any additions or subtractions.

Yet when the Tempter asked whether God's prohibition of eating from the forbidden tree was good and reasonable, Eve said, "We may eat of the fruit of the trees of the garden: But of the fruit of the tree which is in the midst of the garden, God hath said, Ye shall not eat of it, neither shall ye touch it, lest ye die" (Gen 3:2–3). Eve's response represents the first recorded instance of God's Word being distorted. God had not prohibited touching the fruit. He merely forbade eating it. For the very first time, mankind was faced with a crisis of authority. In response, Eve rendered God's Word inaccurately rather than trusting it as the authoritative revelation of her Creator.

Is God's Word authoritative? Can it be trusted? Should it be believed and accepted? Is it accurate and without error? Is it sufficient to meet humanity's emotional, intellectual, and spiritual needs? The Genesis incident ignited a flame of distortion and unbelief that has been burning out of control ever since.

The distorting of God's Word has worsened over the years. This is not to suggest a total absence of preachers and local churches that remain true to

1

God's infallible Word. There are many. I am suggesting, however, that God's Word is being undermined today by preachers who, for practical purposes, deny its sufficiency. Some feel they need to add to or subtract from what the Bible says. As James T. Draper suggests, "The doctrine of the sufficiency of the Scriptures is being undermined in our churches."[1] This undermining occurs, he argues, when Christians fall prey to three dangers:

> The first danger is the error of adding to the Word of God . . . the latest craze among those searching for extrabiblical, private revelation. What is so misleading about this error is that its proponents acknowledge that the Bible is necessary for salvation and service, but they deny that it is sufficient. The replacing of the Word of God is the second danger facing churches today. When the clear teaching of the Bible is replaced with modern psychological theory, the purpose of the church is no longer salvation, but therapy. The third danger may be the most treacherous of all, because it is the least obvious. The displacing of the Word of God occurs when the preaching and teaching of the Bible are relegated to the periphery of the worship of the church. This misstep is harder to detect, because in order to commit this error it is not necessary to do anything to the Bible or to its teachings—just leave them out.[2]

Whether one agrees with Draper's specific observations or not, most Christians will probably concur that God's Word is under attack. It is being undermined by preachers across denominational lines. On any given Sunday, men stand in pulpits across our nation with open Bibles and mouths, muting God's words and inserting their own in its place. Countless thousands have been duped into believing that what is being preached is God's Word when it is merely the personal thoughts and opinions of the preacher. A great need exists to restore textual accuracy and relevance to biblical preaching, particularly in African American pulpits.

The problem of misrepresenting God's Word is not restricted to African Americans or white Americans; it transcends race and culture. It is a problem facing all Christians in all denominations. However, as an African American, I am passionately concerned about the African American pulpit and whether God's Word is treated with the utmost integrity there. African American pulpits desperately need a revival of biblical fidelity and relevance in their approach to

---

[1] James T. Draper Jr. and Kenneth Keathley, *Biblical Authority: The Critical Issue for the Body of Christ* (Nashville, TN: Broadman & Holman Publishers, 2001), 109.

[2] Ibid., 109–10.

preaching. As Thabiti M. Anyabwile notes in *The Decline of African American Theology*:

> As a consequence of theological drift and erosion, the black church now stands in danger of losing its relevance and power to effectively address both the spiritual needs of its communicants and the social and political aspirations of its community.[3]

This book will address four topics related to textual accuracy and relevance in biblical preaching. The first topic to be considered is the crisis necessitating a reemphasis of textual accuracy and relevance in biblical preaching. Segregation and theological training, black liberation theology, and prosperity theology will be discussed. This chapter is not intended to be an exhaustive study of these subjects. Rather, it addresses them as they relate to the overall theme of this work. This chapter will build the foundation upon which the remainder of the book rests and will therefore be the longest.

The second topic to be considered will be the importance of exegesis for biblical and relevant preaching. The definition, importance, and crisis of exegesis will be discussed. An explanation about the building blocks needed to produce sound exegesis will also be explained.

The third topic to be considered is the theology of preaching. The nature of biblical preaching, the ethos of preaching in the African American tradition, and the importance and value of expository preaching will be explained.

The final topic to be considered will be relevance in preaching. The subject of postmodernism will be delineated. In an effort to demonstrate why effectively communicating God's Word in an age of skepticism and relativism is important to all pulpits, input from seasoned Bible expositors will be cited.

---

[3] Thabiti M. Anyabwile, *The Decline of African-American Theology* (Downers Grove, IL: InterVarsity, 2007), 18.

1

The Crisis
Erosion of Biblical Preaching in African American Pulpits

Then the LORD said to me, The prophets prophesy lies in
my name: I sent them not, neither have I commanded them,
neither spake unto them: they prophesy unto you false vision
and divination, and a thing of nought, and the deceit of their
heart . . . I have not sent these prophets, yet they ran: I have
not spoken to them, yet they prophesied. (Jer 14:14; 23:21)

PREACHING has always been central to black church life, with the preacher regarded as a natural leader in the black community.[1] As Olin P. Moyd observes:

The [black] preachers have been the central figures in their churches. Preaching has been the primary element of their worship. And practical theology has been the content and essence in their preaching.[2]

Moyd adds, "Historic African-American preaching was both interpretation and proclamation."[3] Even during slavery, black people found refuge and solace in the preaching they heard each Lord's Day. Preaching provided emotional

[1] Charles V. Hamilton, *The Black Preacher in America* (New York, NY: William Morrow & Company, 1972), 12.
[2] Olin P. Moyd, *The Sacred Art–Preaching and Theology in the African-American Tradition* (Valley Forge, PA: Judson, 1995), 1.
[3] Ibid., 2.

inspiration and was, in a sense, a survival mechanism.[4] While they awaited their emancipation, preaching helped slaves endure the hardships and unjust treatment imposed by their owners. This is why the black preacher was so essential to African American Christians. Lewis V. Baldwin echoes these sentiments: "The single most important figure in the black Christian experience is the black preacher."[5]

Preaching continues to be a mainstay in African American churches. This should come as no surprise to any Bible student since preaching is the method God chose to convey his Word and will to lost humanity. Paul said regarding God's use of preaching that "it pleased God by the foolishness of preaching to save them that believe" (1 Cor 1:21). It is this foolishness of preaching that African Americans need.

However, preaching in some African American pulpits has, over time, evolved and taken a less than conservative approach in its dealing with textual accuracy and relevance. This is a crisis which necessitates a change. Dale Andrews, in *Practical Theology for Black Churches* says, "Through the generations of black preaching, African American folk religion has developed a 'black hermeneutic' for the interpretation and application of the Bible."[6] This "black hermeneutic" has wreaked havoc on African American churches because it manipulates the Bible's intended meaning. The church in America today faces a crisis like no other time in its history. There is therefore a need for biblical accuracy and relevance to be restored to all pulpits, especially African American ones. As we will see, at least three factors have precipitated the decline of biblical preaching among black churches: segregation, black liberation theology, and prosperity theology.

SEGREGATION AND THEOLOGICAL TRAINING

From the beginning of our nation's history, African Americans have endured racism and racial segregation. Racial segregation is born out of an attitude of superiority. A race that considers itself dominant claims the legal and moral right to discriminate against a race it considers inferior. As racial segregation continued its evolution in America, the dominant white race felt duty-bound to discriminate against black people.

---

[4] Hamilton, *The Black Preacher in America*, 37.

[5] Lewis V. Baldwin, "Black Christianity in the South in the Nineteenth Century: It's Development and Character," in *Religion in the South Conference Papers* (Birmingham, AL: Alabama Humanities Foundation, 1986), 19.

[6] Dale P. Andrews, *Practical Theology for Black Churches* (Louisville, KY: Westminster John Knox, 2002), 16.

Behind racial segregation and discrimination was the idea that black people were not fully part of the human race.[7] This idea was especially popular during the days of slavery when blacks inherited at birth a status that excluded them from many privileges normally associated with being human.[8] Generally, slaves were prohibited from learning to read or write for fear they might become intelligent enough to stand up against their masters. A body of laws known as the Slave Codes[9] was enacted to keep slaves in a position of subservience. These laws covered every aspect of life for slaves and inhibited especially their social and intellectual development.

The Slave Codes also affected the religious life of slaves. They were permitted to hear the Bible preached each Lord's Day but only under the strict guardianship of slave owners. They were allowed to attend their owners' churches but had to sit in segregated sections, oftentimes in the upper balconies. Slave owners often encouraged their slaves to attend preaching services because it was thought such religious experiences would make them more docile and cooperative. To nurture cooperation, white preachers would admonish the slaves to obey their masters. Scripture passages like Ephesians 6:5[10] were distorted in an attempt to teach slaves that disobedience to their owners was equivalent to disobeying God himself and would result in severe chastisement.

On occasion slaves were permitted to conduct their own separate worship services held in their slave quarters. The slaves worshiped with singing, praying, and preaching. Since the majority of black preachers could not read or write, their knowledge of the Bible and theology was restricted. Consequently, most of what they preached was based on memory of what they heard from white preachers. They would sometimes even imitate the words and actions of white preachers. Pastor and educator William Banks notes, "The Blacks copied what they saw and heard. Basically, the religion of the plantation Black was a faithful copy of the White man's religion."[11] The messages from these black preachers were emotional, energetic, and connected with the daily struggles, frustrations, and burdens carried by slaves.

---

[7] Peter J. Paris, *The Social Teaching of the Black Churches* (Philadelphia, PA: Fortress, 1985), 4.

[8] Ibid.

[9] John Hope Franklin, *From Slavery to Freedom: A History of Negro Americans* (New York, NY: Alfred A. Knopf, 1974), 140.

[10] "Servants, be obedient to them that are your masters according to the flesh, with fear and trembling, in singleness of your heart, as unto Christ" (Eph 6:5).

[11] William L. Banks, *The History of Black Baptists in the United States* (Philadelphia, PA: The Continental Press, 1987), 36.

The worship experience of slaves was always scrutinized by the slave owners. The black preacher had to be extremely careful not to anger the slave master by the subject matter he preached. As James Harris states,

> During much of slavery, especially during the nineteenth century, black preachers were forbidden by law and custom to preach the gospel, presumably because of the increase in rebellion and insurrections of religious radicals.[12]

Charles Hamilton adds:

> Where the black preacher was permitted to serve the slaves, he was expected by the slaveholders to pacify the slaves and to reconcile them to their lowly lot here on earth. Those who performed that function well, were rewarded by the whites for it.[13]

With the abolition of slavery came a new approach to racism: Jim Crow laws.[14] To protect white rights and interests, laws were passed that encouraged white dominance and kept whites separated from blacks. This legalized racial discrimination in America. The result was the continued repression of black people in a society that measured superiority and inferiority solely on the basis of pigmentation.

In childhood, African Americans learned that the differences between themselves and white people amounted to more than skin color. As William Chafe, Raymond Gavins, and Robert Korstad note:

> Jim Crow meant confronting bitter truths about human nature. . . . Among the most poignant of these realities emerged when African-American children came to understand that blacks and whites were different in the eyes of society. Walking to school, going to

---

[12] James H. Harris, *Preaching Liberation* (Minneapolis, MN: Fortress Press, 1995), 41.

[13] Hamilton, *The Black Preacher in America*, 37.

[14] Linda Barrett Osborne, *Miles To Go For Freedom – Segregation and Civil Rights In The Jim Crow Years* (New York: Abrams Books, 2012), 21; *The World Book Encyclopedia* (Willard, OH: RR Donnelley, 2014), 11:126. The term "Jim Crow" came into common use in the 1800s, when racial segregation was legal in many parts of the southern United States. The term originally referred to a black character in a popular song composed in the 1830s. Thomas "Daddy" Rice, a white actor, had created a song and dance that he performed while pretending to be a black man–Jim Crow. The character Jim Crow embodied popular stereotypes about African Americans. He wore ragged clothes and shoes with holes in them. He was lazy, comical, not too bright, and spoke with an exaggerated accent. "Jim Crow" described the race-based way of life in the South and quickly came to mean "second-class citizen." The idea of "separate but equal" status was intended to pacify the black community while protecting white interests and bolstering the discriminatory practices of whites toward blacks. Most Jim Crow laws were nullified by Supreme Court decisions in the 1950s and 1960s, and the Civil Rights Acts of 1964 and 1968. For additional resources on this topic see Joel Williamson, *The Crucible of Race: Black-White Relations in the American South since Emancipation* (New York: Oxford University Press, 1984) and Steven Hahn, *A Nation Under Our Feet: Black Political Struggles in the Rural South from Slavery to the Great Migration* (Cambridge: Belknap Press, 2005).

the store, playing on rural farms and city sidewalks, black children confronted racial differences in the taunts of white children, in the degrading treatment of black adults, and in their own observations of who was better off than whom. Under such circumstances you just automatically grew up inferior and you had the feeling that white people were better than you.[15]

Discrimination against black people extended to social interactions, housing, employment, and education. Nowhere was the oppression more apparent than in the realm of religious education. Both liberal and conservative institutions resisted integrated classrooms, but some schools closed their doors to blacks altogether. Even after the Supreme Court's 1954 *Brown v. Board of Education* decision, schools like Bob Jones University in Greenville, South Carolina, and Tennessee Temple University in Chattanooga, Tennessee, enforced admission restrictions based on race. The idea that whites were superior to blacks was the accepted norm and white supremacy triumphed in America.

PROBLEMS CREATED BY RACIAL SEGREGATION

Racial segregation led to at least four major problems: degradation of black communities, bitterness toward America, a propensity to embrace the social gospel, and devaluation of human life.

Effect on Black Communities

The first problem created by racial segregation was the degradation of black communities. Due to their denial of the access and opportunity afforded most white Americans, African Americans were relegated to poverty, illiteracy, and a "ghetto" mind-set where hopelessness and despair prevailed. African Americans had to endure, at times, horrendous living conditions just to survive. In the majority of predominantly African American neighborhoods, crime, drug trafficking, gang violence, unemployment, and deplorable living conditions prevailed. Many of these neighborhoods had little if any public transportation and few grocery stores or hospitals. It is a sad reality but fifty years after the civil rights race riots in Watts, Chicago, Detroit, and Cleveland, many urban neighborhoods are still in disarray and people still live in hopelessness.

To make matters worse, the response of government officials to the pressing needs of black neighborhoods typically was slower and less enthusiastic

---

[15] William H. Chafe, Raymond Gavins, and Robert Korstad, eds., *Remembering Jim Crow: African-Americans Tell About Life in the Segregated South* (New York, NY: The New York Press, 2001), 2–3.

then their repose to white communities. Even today, in the majority of white communities, government officials don't tolerate dilapidated buildings or vacant lots. Not so in the majority of African American neighborhoods. Many of those neighborhoods look strikingly similar to the way they did the morning after the riots of the 1960s.

Bitterness toward America

The second problem created by racial segregation was bitterness toward America. Many African Americans believed the Founding Fathers' claim that "all men are created equal" was intended only as a statement about whites. African Americans theorized that when our nation's forefathers fashioned that statement, black people were probably not included in their thought processes. As evidence, they noted that several men who signed the Declaration of Independence owned slaves. Frustration with the racism that apparently informed the writing of America's founding documents became the impetus for creating cultural genres that represented African Americans. Disappointed with their suppressed surroundings, African Americans often fell into despair, which generated bitterness.

From the root of this bitterness, the Nation of Islam and the Black Panther Party emerged. Both groups were extreme in their separatist ideologies and sought retaliation against white segregationists. Their members were willing to become modern-day martyrs if that's what it took to thwart the segregationist agenda. Yet neither group was able to accomplish its intended goals. Hatred and violence only begat more hatred and violence.

Other groups sprung up which had the same goal of liberation but a different philosophical approach. Groups like the Southern Christian Leadership Conference (SCLC), Congress of Racial Equality (CORE), Student Nonviolent Coordinating Committee (SNCC), and the National Association for the Advancement of Colored People (NAACP) were all organized to advocate racial equality while placating a growing number of black people demanding immediate justice by any means necessary. The philosophical approach of these groups centered on achieving liberation through non-violence. There were obvious merits to the approach of these groups. If nothing else, they provided African Americans a heightened sense of expectation for personal liberties. Negatively, these groups at times fostered an "us versus them" mentality that helped justify racial separation and contributed more to racial segregation than desegregation.

Educational Disparity and Political Activism

The third problem was a propensity among black preachers to seek social justice through political activism. These preachers believed the gospel's trans- formative power can—indeed must—be applied to contemporary social, cultural, and political structures. Victimized by racism, the black church in America was set on a course that led it into heretical teachings. Even after African Americans began attending white institutions, many still looked to political activism as a means to genuine equality. Sadly, the gospel occasion- ally got lost in the shuffle.

The church offered African Americans solace from racial suppression as activism became the focus of much preaching. The message was one of lib- eration and reform as proponents focused on transforming society. To leave the persecuted and underprivileged paddling upstream against their demor- alizing conditions without any hope of reaching the safe shores of liberation was unconscionable. Consequently, activist preachers focused on alleviating racism, sexism, and poverty without stressing traditional Christian teaching about repentance and faith in Christ as Lord and Savior.

There were, of course, some African American preachers who looked for other ways to address their grievances. Consider John McNeal Jr., founder and pastor of the Atlanta Bible Baptist Church. In 1964 McNeal became the first African American male to graduate from Grace Theological Seminary in Wynona Lake, Indiana. Following his graduation, Grace Seminary made intentional efforts to attract and admit African American men. Other schools like Dallas Theological Seminary in Dallas, Texas; Baptist Bible College in Springfield, Missouri; and The Southern Baptist Theological Seminary in Lou- isville, Kentucky, have for several decades been proactive in recruiting Afri- can Americans. Still, racial segregation prevented many black ministers from receiving adequate theological training needed to fulfill their God-given call to "preach the word" (2 Tim 4:2). The results were devastating.

Consider the theology of our nation's most prolific liberation preacher. The late Martin Luther King Jr. King received his theological training from three liberal institutions: Morehouse College in Atlanta, Georgia (where in 1948 he received his bachelor of arts in sociology), Crozer Seminary in Ches- ter, Pennsylvania (where he received his bachelor of divinity in 1951), and Boston University's School of Theology in Boston, Massachusetts (where in 1955 he received his doctorate in systematic theology).

As a result of his training, King's theology was liberal in nature. It bears repeating that in the minds of many black people, conservative theologians were suspect because they appealed to God's Word to defend slavery, promote white supremacy, and champion racial segregation. Thus, the writings of Reinhold Niebuhr[16] and Karl Marx[17] helped shape King's theological convictions.

Of course, King's theology also drew from traditional Christian orthodoxy. He appealed to the Sermon on the Mount and its emphasis on practically demonstrating Christian love. This became the foundation for his philosophy of nonviolence. King summarized this philosophy by saying, "It was Jesus of Nazareth that stirred the Negroes to protest with the creative weapon of love."[18] According to King's interpretation of Christianity, every Christian was duty bound to love all people regardless of race or national origin. This unshackled people from the chains of hatred, racism, and retaliation, and it essentially set them free to do what God had called them to do. This practical side of Christianity is what philosopher Cornel West called "being free to love across the board."[19] King became the champion of nonviolent resistance, which many believed was the most potent weapon available to African Americans in their struggle for freedom.

Along with the Sermon on the Mount, however, King was influenced deeply by the father of the social gospel, Walter Rauschenbusch—particularly his book *Christianity and the Social Crisis*. As King noted:

> I came early to Walter Rauschenbusch's *Christianity and the Social Crisis*, which left an indelible imprint on my thinking by giving me a theological basis for the social concern which had already grown up in me as a result of my early experiences. It is my conviction ever since reading Rauschenbusch that any religion that professes concern for souls of men and is not equally concerned about the slums that damn them, the economic conditions that strangle them, and the social conditions that cripple them is a spiritually moribund religion only waiting for the day to be buried. It well has been said: A religion that ends with the individual, ends.[20]

King's concept of the gospel of Jesus Christ dealt with the whole person—not only his soul but his body also, not only his spiritual well-being but

---

[16] Karl Paul Reinhold Niebuhr (1892–1971) was an American theologian and seminary professor. He was neo-orthodox in his theological convictions and a Christian realist in his ethics.

[17] Karl Heinrich Marx (1818–1883) was a German philosopher who furthered the causes of socialism and communism. His theories about the development of societal life became known as "Marxism."

[18] Clayborne Carson, ed., *The Autobiography of Martin Luther King, Jr.* (New York, NY: Grand Central, 1998), 67.

[19] Cornel West, *Hope on a Tightrope* (New York, NY: Smiley, 2008), 84.

[20] Carson, *The Autobiography of Martin Luther King, Jr.*, 18.

also his material well-being. The whole idea of social change intrigued King. He quickly embraced the social gospel movement even though many of its supporters deemphasized salvation, declared traditional Christian orthodoxy outdated, and instead focused on helping the poor apart from gospel preaching.[21] One can only imagine the impact King might have had on the African American church had he been strongly influenced by theological conservatism. King's brilliant mind, grasp of the English language, and oratory skills, would have made him an excellent expository preacher.

Devaluating Human Life

The fourth problem created by racial segregation is the most destructive of all: It distorts God's Word and devalues human life. If someone believes one race is superior to another, then Genesis 1–11 must be distorted or disregarded because these chapters are crucial in laying the foundation for the Christian's convictions about creation and the equality of all men regardless of ethnicity.

When God said, "Let us make man in our image, after our likeness" (Gen 1:26), to whom was he referring? Was he referring to a specific ethnic group? Is it plausible that in the Genesis record, God was referring exclusively to one particular race of people? Of course not! It would be ludicrous to even suggest such a thing. As an African American preacher, the author has encountered people who, by their racist attitudes and actions, seem to have been taught that God created whites to dominate all other races and cursed blacks to be subservient. This teaching is perhaps derived, in particular, from poor exegesis of Genesis 9, the biblical account of Noah's drunkenness and the disgraceful act perpetrated by his son Ham, the father of Canaan.

> And Noah began *to be* an husbandman, and he planted a vineyard: And he drank of the wine, and was drunken; and he was uncovered within his tent. And Ham, the father of Canaan, saw the nakedness of his father, and told his two brethren without. And Shem and Japheth took a garment, and laid *it* upon both their shoulders, and went backward, and covered the nakedness of their father; and their faces were backward, and they saw not their father's nakedness. And Noah awoke from his wine, and knew what his younger son had done unto him. And he said, Cursed be Canaan; a servant of servants shall he be unto his brethren. And he said, blessed be the Lord God of Shem; and Canaan shall be his servant. God shall enlarge Japheth,

---

[21] Jessica McElrath, *The Everything Martin Luther King Jr. Book* (Avon, MA: Adams Media, 2008), 34.

and he shall dwell in the tents of Shem; and Canaan shall be his
servant. (Gen 9:20–27)

This narrative has been debated by theologians for centuries. Questions
have arisen such as, "Why did Noah curse Canaan when Ham had committed
the sin?" and "Is the black race cursed by God?" Is a correct understanding of
this narrative possible? The obvious answer is yes. Several observations contribute to a correct understanding. First, it should be noted that Ham's actions
probably were not homosexual in nature. If Ham had engaged in sexual relations with his father, we might expect the Hebrew to be translated "he uncov-
ered his father's nakedness."[22]

Second, Noah spoke prophetically of the nation of Canaanites that would
come from Ham through his son Canaan. This was a prediction that the Canaanites would be servants to the Shemites and Japhethites. Looking through the
lens of his omniscience, God knew the Canaanites would be characterized by
idolatry, immorality, and drunkenness. He therefore judged them.

Third, nothing in the text makes reference to skin color. Some proponents
of white supremacy believe the curse entailed, in part, having dark skin. However, Canaan was not a black man and neither were any of his descendants. For
countless African Americans who have been taught to hate themselves because
their lips are too broad or their hair too textured, a correct interpretation of
Genesis 9 is liberating.[23]

Racial segregationists' attempts to use God's Word to justify their claims
have all proven futile. Faulty exegesis can breed racism and belief in evolution, both of which demean human life. God is the originator of all human
existence. He created all men equal. No man is better than another man, and
no race is superior to another. Races, cultures, backgrounds, and people are
different, not superior or inferior. For any preacher to stand before God's people and attempt to biblically justify racial superiority, hatred, or segregation,
is mishandling God's Word. Those who have done so should either repent of
their sin or vacate their pulpits.

A BIBLICAL VIEW OF RACE

Relevant, biblical preaching can restore to Christ's body a theology and
practice that exalts God as the creator of all men. It can also promote proper

---

[22] John F. Walvoord and Roy B. Zuck, eds., *The Bible Knowledge Commentary: Old Testament* (Colorado Springs, CO: David C. Cook, 1985), 41.

[23] Wallace Charles Smith, *The Church in the Life of the Black Family* (Valley Forge, PA:
Judson, 1985), 54.

race relations in the church. Psalm 139 is an excellent resource for cultivating a biblical worldview regarding race relations. The entire chapter is devoted to God's omniscience, omnipresence, and omnipotence. In verses 13–18, David extols God's power in creating man by saying,

> For thou hast possessed my reins: thou hast covered me in my mother's womb. I will praise thee; for I am fearfully and wonderfully made: marvelous are thy works; and that my soul knoweth right well. My substance was not hid from thee, when I was made in secret, and curiously wrought in the lowest parts of the earth. Thine eyes did see my substance, yet being unperfect; and in thy book all my members were written, which in continuance were fashioned, when as yet there was none of them. How precious also are thy thoughts unto me, O God! How great is the sum of them! If I should count them, they are more in number than the sand: when I awake, I am still with thee. (Ps 139:13–18)

These verses provide a basis for a biblical worldview as it relates to race discrimination, and two truths in this passage are noteworthy for thinking about race.

God Is Responsible for Man's Creation

God established the natural processes of reproduction and created each man in his mother's womb. This is such an amazing phenomenon that it prompted David to break out in praise that he was "fearfully and wonderfully made" (v. 14). This truth imparts dignity and worth to each person's life. Regardless of ethnicity, background, or setting, every person is uniquely handcrafted by God, and to suggest otherwise is equivalent to suggesting that God is incompetent.

There is unity and diversity in God's creation. Humankind was created as a diverse population. Each person *looks, thinks, and acts different from every other*; and yet humankind was also created with unity. Every human shares the same anatomical and spiritual structure. Regardless of ethnicity, each person's material body and spiritual makeup is like that of every other. All men have indeed been created equal. And all mankind is in need of God's love and forgiveness offered through his Son Jesus Christ.

God Is Responsible for Man's Ethnicity

The second noteworthy truth is closely associated with the first. In verse 16 David exclaims, "Thine eyes did see my substance, yet being unperfect;

and in thy book all my members were written, which in continuance were fashioned, when as yet there was none of them." The psalmist is teaching his readers that God superintends every aspect of every person's creation. God has preordained all the days of each person's life before they are even born.

This truth serves as a reminder that a person's ethnicity is determined by God. It is also a reminder that body structure, hair texture, and facial features are determined by God. This functions as a great equalizer. segregation and racism would be eliminated if everyone accepted the fact that everyone has been "fashioned" according to God's good pleasure.

African American pulpits must return to the accurate interpretation and application of God's Word. It is from the Bible that African Americans learn they were created in the image and likeness of God. It is in the Bible that they find reason to applaud and appreciate their rich heritage and existence as black people.

BLACK LIBERATION THEOLOGY

The second topic to examine and evaluate is the dangerous teaching known as black liberation theology. Since its inception, black liberation theology has challenged the white racism rooted throughout American public and private realms. It has held white society accountable and exposed cultural, political, and economic injustice.[24]

Proponents of this theology saw the traditional white-oriented church as a racist institution that was only concerned with the status quo. Emphasis was therefore placed on the black church as a means of liberating black people from the injustices they were being forced to endure.

James H. Cone[25] is regarded as the chief progenitor of the black liberation theology movement. Cone suggests that "unlike white theology, which tends to make the Jesus-event an abstract, unembodied idea, black theology believes that the black community itself is precisely where Jesus is at work."[26]

---

[24] Dale P. Andrews, *Practical Theology for Black Churches* (Louisville, KY: Westminster John Knox, 2002), 83.

[25] Anyabwile, *The Decline of African-American Theology*, 48–49. James H. Cone grew up during the 1940s and early '50s—the age of Jim Crow. The faith he acquired from attending Macedonia AME Church in Bearden, Arkansas, provided the impetus for his stand against the prevailing belief that blacks were less than whites. Cone struggled with the seeming hypocrisy and contradiction of white churches that claimed to love the Lord and welcome all people but practiced segregation. Cone's theology was developed from the struggle for racial freedom among black people in America. Cone found Christian inspiration in the activist theology of Martin Luther King Jr., and a renewed appreciation of his blackness in the critique of Malcolm X and the Black Power movement he spawned.

[26] James H. Cone, *A Black Theology of Liberation* (Maryknoll, NY: Orbis Books, 1990), 5.

From its inception, black liberation theology has viewed the Jesus-event[27] as a black event, an event of liberation from white oppressors and their inhumane treatment of black people. For Cone and his colleagues, liberation is the sole content of biblical theology. Cone says quite unapologetically that Christian theology is a theology of liberation. It is a rational study of the being of God in the world in light of the existential situation of an oppressed community, relating to forces of liberation to the essence of the gospel, which is Jesus Christ.[28]

Black liberation theology originated from the oppression experienced by African Americans. Created to emphasize the liberation of people from adverse sociopolitical and economic conditions, black liberation theology is, as Cone described it, "that theology which arises out of the need to articulate the significance of Black presence in a hostile white world."[29] Cone viewed the black experience as dominated by humiliation and suffering, conditions from which all blacks needed to be liberated.

Cone's philosophy of liberation does not denote the liberation of a person's soul from sin's curse as God's Word clearly explains in Galatians 3:13.[30] Rather, he is referring to people being liberated from their social, economic, and racial suppression. It is Cone's premise that "Christian theology can only mean black theology, a theology that speaks of God as related to black liberation."[31] Cone adds:

> If we agree that the gospel is the proclamation of God's liberating
> activity, that the Christian community is an oppressed community
> that participates in that activity, and that theology is the discipline
> arising from within the Christian community as it seeks to develop
> adequate language for its relationship to God's liberation, then black
> theology is Christian theology.[32]

Black liberation theology holds that to be authentic, the gospel of Jesus Christ must relate to the pain and suffering of being black in a white racist society. In service of this goal, black liberation theologians reinterpret two key Christian doctrines: revelation and the person and work of Christ.

---

[27] The "Jesus-event" the Bible speaks of is his coming to "seek and to save that which was lost" (Luke 19:10).

[28] Cone, *A Black Theology of Liberation*, 1.

[29] James H. Cone, "Black Consciousness and the Black Church," *Christianity and Crisis* 30, no. 18 (November 1970): 23.

[30] "Christ hath redeemed us from the curse of the law, being made a curse for us: for it is written, cursed is everyone that hangeth on a tree" (Gal 3:13).

[31] Cone, *A Black Theology of Liberation*, 9.

[32] Ibid.

Revelation and Black Liberation Theology

For these theologians, revelation is more than divine self-disclosure. It is specifically God's self-disclosure to humankind in the context of liberation.[33] Because white racists can accept the historic view that revelation is God's self-disclosure, black liberation theologians revise the doctrines of general and special revelation in light of their emphasis on black liberation. For black liberation theologians, the self-disclosure of God signifies that he identifies with and will eventually emancipate African Americans from death-dealing political, economic, and social structures.[34] Any supposed revelation of God that does not reference his work of liberating oppressed people is to be considered as anti-biblical. Cone states: "[I]n the zeal to be biblical, we cannot lose sight of the contemporary situation and what this situation means to the oppressed of the land."[35]

The exodus paradigm becomes essential to black liberation theology. It becomes the exegetical lens for understanding God's liberating message for the oppressed that can be traced throughout the entire Old Testament and corroborated by the New Testament. In the exodus narrative, God revealed himself as Israel's warrior liberator. Through a series of miracles, God emancipated his people from oppression and suffering at the hands of the Egyptians. Then God established an eternal covenant with Israel thus expressing his continual identification with them as their liberator. To remind his people that he was their eternal liberator, God repeatedly said, "I am the Lord thy God, which brought thee out of the land of Egypt, from the house of bondage" (Deut 5:6, 15; Lev 26:13).

In similar fashion, black liberation theology asserts that God's covenant with African Americans is his identification with them as their great emancipator. As the Bible reveals God as Israel's liberator from oppression and slavery, it also reveals him as liberator of all the oppressed. As Cone states, "There is no revelation of God without a condition of oppression which develops into a situation of liberation."[36]

In black liberation theology, God becomes the warrior liberator of African Americans. This is the pivotal point for black liberation theology. Warren H. Stewart Sr. says, "No other point in black theology has been so central to all

---

[33] Ibid., 45.
[34] Ibid.
[35] Ibid.
[36] Ibid.

of its noted advocates."[37] Black liberation theology is therefore a theology of freedom, a theology where oppressed black people can find hope and strength to endure, knowing that God had been actively involved in the liberation of the Hebrew children, and thus, more than likely, he would take an active part in the liberation of black people from their oppression.[38]

Jesus and Black Liberation Theology

Jesus is essential to the belief system of black liberation theology. As Cone states,

> To speak of the Christian gospel is to speak of Jesus Christ who is the content of its message and without whom Christianity ceases to be. Therefore the answer to the question "What is the essence of Christianity?" can be given in the two words: Jesus Christ.[39]

With the growth of racial discrimination and segregation in America, a new approach to Christology ensued. Black liberation theologians argued that racism in America had pre-conditioned people to suppose Jesus was a white man with blonde hair and blue eyes. How can a white Jesus relate to the struggles, pain, and agony of black people, they asked? The answer was clear: He can't. To contest the preposterous notion of a white Jesus, black liberation theologians emphasized the humanity of Jesus. A new Christology emerged highlighting the relational side of Jesus.

Since the Jesus being preached by most white preachers had little relevance to black people and their condition, a Jesus who could relate to the racial, cultural, and social context of black people was required. A Jesus who knew first-hand about people's struggles was necessary. Jesus needed to be portrayed as a friend to whom African Americans could turn during their times of distress. Liberation theologians proposed that Jesus must be presented as personally identifying with the disinherited.[40] It was also proposed that for people to understand Christianity, they must "see it through a black perspective."[41]

---

[37] Warren H. Stewart Sr., *Interpreting God's Word in Black Preaching* (Valley Forge, PA: Judson, 1984), 17.

[38] Ibid., 18.

[39] Cone, *A Black Theology of Liberation*, 110.

[40] Anyabwile, *The Decline of African-American Theology*, 152, 158. "Disinherited" was the term used by Howard Thurman (1900–1981) to promote his view of Jesus's work on earth as standing with all the downtrodden of every generation. Thurman argued that the historical Jesus and his context resembled the context of American Negroes of his day. See Thurman, *Jesus and the Disinherited* (Boston, MA: Beacon, 1976).

[41] Hamilton, *The Black Preacher in America*, 147.

Over time, some African Americans became enamored with the thought of a "black Jesus," a "black Messiah," or a "black God." Cone attempted to substantiate his claim that God is black by saying,

> The blackness of God, and everything implied by it in a racist society, is the heart of Black Theology's doctrine of God. There is no place in Black Theology for a colorless God in a society when people suffer precisely because of their color. The black theologian must reject any conception of God which stifles black self-determination by picturing God as a God of all peoples. Either God is identified with the oppressed to the point that their experience becomes his or he is a God of racism. The blackness of God means that God has made the oppressed condition his own condition. This is the essence of the biblical revelation.[42]

United Church of Christ preacher Albert Cleage defended his participation in the civil rights movement by stating, "Jesus was a revolutionary black leader, a Zealot, seeking to lead a Black Nation to freedom."[43]

Black liberation theologians believed that preaching Jesus was equivalent to preaching liberation. Jesus was the oppressed one whose entire earthly existence was bound up with the oppressed. When preaching about Jesus the liberator, much emphasis was placed on his life and ministry and his identification with what Roberts called "the least, the lonely, and the lost."[44]

Luke 4:18–19[45] emerged as a proof text of black liberation theologians. The setting in Luke's gospel is Jesus in the synagogue, standing and reading from the prophet Isaiah. Jesus defines his earthly ministry as being divinely energized by God's Spirit to work among the downcast and downtrodden of his day, thus bringing God the Father into people's minds and hearts. Black liberation theologians use this text to portray Jesus as a revolutionary leader focused on confronting the problems that afflict humanity.

To further demonstrate Jesus's affinity for the disinherited, black liberation theologians emphasized that Jesus was born a Jew. By training, background, and religion, Jesus belonged to the Jewish minority. As a racial minority, he

---

[42] Cone, *A Black Theology of Liberation*, 120–21, 124.

[43] Albert B. Cleage Jr., *The Black Messiah* (New York, NY: Sheed and Ward, 1968), 4.

[44] J. Deotis Roberts, *Africentric Christianity: A Theological Appraisal for Ministry* (Valley Forge, PA: Judson, 2000), 63.

[45] "The Spirit of the Lord is upon me, because he hath anointed me to preach the gospel to the poor; he hath sent me to heal the brokenhearted, to preach deliverance to the captives, and recovering of sight to the blind, to set at liberty them that are bruised" (Luke 4:18).

knew firsthand what it was like to be viewed as unequal by the dominant group. Jesus was therefore fully qualified to relate to the needs of black Americans.[46]

But Jesus was not only a Jew; he was a "poor Jew."[47] Jesus's earthly parents' inability to provide a lamb for the sacrifice has been used to demonstrate the impoverished conditions of his earthly life (Luke 2:22–24).[48] Thurman, though not himself a black liberation theologian, noted, "The economic predicament with which he was identified in birth placed him initially with the great mass of men on earth. The masses of people are poor."[49] Jesus's life was of such deprivation that the prophet Isaiah could say of him, "He is despised and rejected of men; a man of sorrows, and acquainted with grief" (Isa 53:3). From this new Christology came messages of hope in the midst of despair, and African Americans felt Jesus could fully identify with their plight.

Problems Associated with Black Liberation Theology

At least three problems associated with black liberation theology necessitate a reemphasis on biblical preaching among black churches. First, it is a threat to biblical Christianity. It twists, distorts, and ultimately denies the gospel of Jesus Christ. It ignores man's spiritual need by concentrating exclusively on his social or physical needs. It takes the simple message of biblical salvation and mixes political and social ideologies into it.

Second, black liberation theology deemphasizes the person and work of the Lord Jesus Christ. While stressing Jesus's humble background and association with the least, the lonely, and the lost, His true mission to earth is eclipsed. Without question, Jesus loves society's social, economic, and political outcasts. However, as he states, his primary mission was "to seek and to save that which is lost" (Luke 19:10).

The message of black liberation theology, though inspiring to some and challenging to hatemongers, lacks spiritual gravitas. When divorced from Jesus's mission of redeeming sinners, his compassion for society's outcasts loses much of its significance. Jesus never claimed his mission was to liberate

---

[46] This idea was drawn from Howard Thurman, though Thurman himself was not a black liberation theologian. See Thurman, *Jesus and the Disinherited* (Boston, MA: Beacon, 1976), 32.

[47] Ibid., 17.

[48] "And when the days of her purification according to the law of Moses were accomplished, they brought him to Jerusalem, to present him to the Lord; (As it is written in the law of the Lord, Every male that openeth the womb shall be called holy to the Lord;) And to offer a sacrifice according to that which is said in the law of the Lord, A pair of turtledoves, or two young pigeons" (Luke 2:22–24).

[49] Thurman, *Jesus and the Disinherited*, 17.

mankind from social, economic, or political injustices. Rather, his mission was to liberate man from the penalty and power of sin. Once liberated from his sin, a man's entire outlook is transformed. He now has the capacity, through the indwelling Holy Spirit, to obey the second greatest commandment which is to "love thy neighbor as thyself" (Matt 22:39).

The third problem associated with black liberation theology is that it contributes to the segregation of Christian churches. It has alienated black Christians from their white brothers and sisters in Christ. The reality that the eleven o'clock hour on Sunday morning is the most segregated hour of the week cannot be contested. In contrast, heaven is racially desegregated, and God has commanded his people to pray, "Thy kingdom come. Thy will be done in earth, as it is in heaven" (Matt 6:10). All Christians should be praying for and promoting unity in the body of Christ. When Jesus Christ established the church, which is his body, his desire was that racial and social barriers be eradicated and all Christians become one in Him irrespective of race or national origin. Writing to the churches in the Galatian region, Paul insists:

> For as many of you as have been baptized into Christ have put on Christ. There is neither Jew nor Greek, there is neither bond nor free, there is neither male nor female: for ye are all one in Christ Jesus. And if ye be Christ's, then are ye Abraham's seed, and heirs according to the promise. (Gal 3:28)

Accurate portrayal of the biblical text in preaching is necessary for the true gospel of Christ to be understood. It is also necessary so that Christians can experience a little heaven on earth by engaging in desegregated worship. God is spirit and we are commanded to worship him "in spirit and in truth" (John 4:24). Theological oneness is a prerequisite to worshipping according to truth. There can be no genuine unity without it.

PROSPERITY THEOLOGY

Another impediment to biblical preaching in black churches is the heretical teaching known as "prosperity theology." This teaching has also been called the "Word of Faith" movement. Its basic teaching is that God rewards faithfulness with good health and material wealth. This has quickly become one of the most captivating messages in churches across our nation, with an impact transcending racial and denominational lines. Advocates such as Joel Osteen of Lakewood Church in Houston, Texas, T. D. Jakes of the Potter's House in Dallas, Texas, Frederick K. C. Price of Crenshaw Christian Center in

Inglewood, California, and Creflo Dollar of World Changers Ministries near Atlanta, Georgia, all expound this message.

Admittedly, these preachers say financial wealth is not the only blessing God brings to his children.[50] Still, their ideology maligns the person and work of our Lord Jesus Christ and distorts the gospel. While they claim to preach the full gospel, in reality their message is what God condemns as being "a different gospel."[51]

The belief system of this movement varies to some extent among its proponents. But there seems to be some uniformity among their teachings on physical health and economic wealth.

Physical Health and Sickness

The movement's philosophy of health was influenced by metaphysical mind science groups such as Christian Science, the Unity School of Christianity and the Church of Religious Science.[52] The prosperity gospel's view of health was summarized by Benny Hinn, one of the movement's most outspoken preachers:

> The healing power of God is present in us; God, the source of life, the creator, is with us forever. In Him we live, in Him we have eternal life; God's greatest desire for the Church of Jesus Christ is that we be in total and perfect health.[53]

Some supporters of this teaching believe any acknowledgment of sickness opens the door to satanic control and medicine is a crutch for the spiritually immature. They also claim the atoning work of Jesus Christ yielded physical healing, and that all diseases are healed by Christ's supposed atonement in hell, not his physical death on the cross. To validate these claims, prosperity gospel preachers appeal to three key Scriptures: Isaiah 53:5 ("The chastisement of our peace was upon him; and with his stripes we are healed"), 1 Peter 2:24 ("by whose stripes ye were healed"), and Matthew 8:17 ("That it might

---

[50] Jeffery B. Bowens, *Prosperity Gospel: Prosperity Gospel and Its Effect on the 21st Century Church* (Bloomington, IN: Xlibris, 2012), 42.

[51] When rebuking the Galatian believers for quickly deserting the true message of the gospel Paul said, "I marvel that ye are so soon removed from him that called you into this grace of Christ unto another gospel: Which is not another; but there be some that trouble you, and would pervert the gospel of Christ" (Gal 1:6–7). Paul makes it known that "another gospel" is in reality "another gospel of a different kind," and therefore not the true gospel.

[52] D. R. McConnell, *A Different Gospel* (Peabody, MA: Hendrickson, 1995), 166, quoted in Richard Abanes, "The Word Faith Movement," and in Walter Martin's, *The Kingdom of the Cults* (Minneapolis, MN: Bethany House, 1977), 279.

[53] Benny Hinn, *Rise and Be Healed* (Orlando, FL: Celebration, 1991), 44.

be fulfilled which was spoken by Esaias the prophet saying, Himself took our infirmaties, and bare our sicknesses").

Again, Hinn's explanation is representative of the movement:

> The Bible declares that the work of Christ (healing) was done 2,000 years ago. God is not going to heal you today: He healed you 2,000 years ago. All you have to do today is receive your healing by faith.[54]

Closely linked to healing is what this movement calls "positive confession," the belief that words have creative power and what people say determines, to some extent, what happens to them. In positive confession, healing and material prosperity are generated by right thinking, right believing, and right confession. It is supposed that people are not being healed because they are thinking wrongly. Three reasons are given for this: first, sickness and disease supposedly are spiritual, not physical; second, a true believer allegedly should never be sick; and third, negative confession purportedly produces sickness.

Positive confession promoters appeal to a portion of Ephesians 5:23 to justify their claims: "and he is the savior of the body." In order for Christians to receive their healing, prosperity gospel preachers say they must positively confess that Christ is the savior of their bodies. When Christians worry or complain about an illness, they forfeit their right to the perfect healing redemption of Christ. The so-called "granddaddy of the Faith teachers"[55] Kenneth Hagin once said:

> I believe that it is the plan of God our Father, that no believer should ever be sick. It is not the will of God my Father that we should suffer with cancer and other dreaded diseases, which bring pain and anguish. No! It is God's will that we be healed.[56]

Hagin, ironically, died from cardiovascular disease in 2003.

Economic Wealth

In addition to their teaching about physical healing, prosperity gospel preachers have much to say about economic wealth. As Hagin put it:

---

[54] Ibid.

[55] Sherry Andrews, "Kenneth Hagin: Keeping the Faith," *Charisma* (October 1981), 24.

[56] Kenneth Hagin, *The Father's Provision* (Word of Faith, August 1977), 9, as quoted in D. R. McConnell's *A Different Gospel*, 157, 168.

> Jesus Christ's atonement has redeemed us from the curse of poverty. This is made a reality because of God's promises to Abraham. Abraham's blessings belong to us. It doesn't belong only to the physical descendants of Abraham; it belongs to us! God promised Abraham that He was going to make him rich. Do you mean that God is going to make us all rich? Yes, that's what I mean. By rich I mean having a full supply. Praise God, there is a full supply in Christ.[57]

Prosperity theology argues that wealth is the divine right of all Christians, accessible in proportion to their level of faith. The believer's faith connection to Abraham puts all the spiritual and physical blessings promised him at their immediate disposal. As T. D. Jakes notes, "Faith is the catalyst that accelerates the divine transfer of wealth to us as believers in Christ Jesus. . . . It motivates God to release His resources on our behalf, and conditions us to receive them."[58]

Two Scriptures commonly used to support the prosperity gospel teaching on wealth are 3 John 2 ("Beloved, I wish above all things that thou mayest prosper and be in health, even as thy soul prospereth") and Luke 6:38 ("Give, and it shall be given unto you; good measure, pressed down, and shaken together, and running over, shall men give into your bosom. For with the same measure that ye mete withal it shall be measured to you again"). Both verses are interpreted as guaranteeing economic prosperity to those who follow God's law.

Nowhere is the heretical nature of the prosperity movement more apparent than its teaching on Christ's incarnation. Many prosperity preachers present a Jesus who looks remarkably like themselves. John Avanzia, for example, presents a Jesus who "is decked out in designer clothes, lives in a big house, has a huge donor base, and has so much money that He needs a treasurer."[59] Another noted supporter of this teaching, Frederick Price, falsely teaches that since Jesus was financially wealthy, believers should be wealthy as well. Price stated:

> The whole point is I'm trying to get you out of the malaise of thinking that Jesus and His disciples were poor, and then relating that to your thinking that you, a child of God have to follow Jesus. The Bible says that he left us an example that we should follow His

---

[57] Kenneth Hagin, *Redeemed from Poverty, Sickness and Spiritual Death* (Tulsa, OK: RHEMA Bible Church, 1997), 9–12.

[58] T. D. Jakes, *Life Overflowing: 6 Pillars for Abundant Living* (Minneapolis, MN: Bethany House, 2008), 15.

[59] John Avanzia, *Praise the Lord* program on TBN (September 15, 1988) and *Believer's Voice of Victory* program on TBN (January 20, 1991).

steps. That's the reason why I drive a Rolls Royce. I'm following Jesus' steps.[60]

Prosperity theology thrives on the idea that wealth is gained in proportion to one's giving to prosperity gospel ministries. This is referred to as "seed planting." Based on the agricultural system of seeding, the concept is an unbiblical extension of the principle that a person reaps what he sows: the more "seed of faith" money a person gives, the greater the return. Promoters of this teaching believe that when a person sows his "seed of faith" money, God creates an atmosphere of perpetual blessing for that person. If people will give their money to the church, the televangelist, or to certain preachers, God supposedly will multiply it back to them 30, 60, or 100 times. This teaching feeds upon a prevailing covetous mentality.

The prosperity theology movement has swept across our nation like a hurricane, leaving in its path broken hearts, broken dreams, and, worst of all, distrust in God. It appears the only ones profiting from this movement are the preachers who endorse and expound on it, with their fabulous homes, designer clothing, fancy automobiles, and enormous bank accounts.

Sad to say, many African American preachers propound the baseless rhetoric of prosperity theologians. Thankfully though, God's Word explains why biblical preaching needs to be restored.

False Assumption Regarding Physical Health

First, the assumption that physical health is guaranteed by Christ's atoning work contradicts biblical teaching. Kenneth Copeland's remarks summarize the movement's beliefs on sickness and health. Copeland said:

> Adam's sin not only got God thrown off planet earth, but also resulted in a satanic nature for Adam. Ever since then, mankind has been susceptible to sin, sickness, suffering, and death; however, the basic principle of the Christian life is to know that God put our sin, sickness, disease, sorrow, grief and poverty on Christ at Calvary. For Him to put any of this on us now would be a miscarriage of justice. Jesus was made a curse for us so that we can receive the blessing of Abraham.[61]

But what exactly does the Bible teach on the subject of sickness? First, it should be noted first that prosperity gospel preachers are correct regarding the

---

[60] Frederick K. C. Price, *Ever Increasing Faith* program on TBN (December 9, 1990).

[61] Kenneth Copeland, *The Troublemaker* (Fort Worth, TX: Copeland Ministries, 1970), 6.

origin of sickness and death. Due to Adam's sin in the garden of Eden, mankind has been inflicted with a curse. According to Romans 8:22–23,[62] this curse has affected the entire creation, which now groans and suffers. This groaning includes our physical bodies, which experience sickness, suffering, and death due to Adam's willful disobedience. Both the righteous and unrighteous share this reality.

Second, and to an extent in keeping with the teaching of prosperity gospel advocates, some sickness is directly related to personal or corporate sin. The apostle Paul reminded the Church at Corinth that their misplaced values, pride, and unconfessed sins had physical consequences for their bodies. With reference to the Corinthians' flippant attitude regarding the Lord's Supper Paul said:

> For he that eateth and drinketh unworthily, eateth and drinketh damnation to himself, not discerning the Lord's body. For this cause many are weak and sickly among you, and many sleep. (1 Cor 11:29–30)

Partaking of the Lord's Supper with unconfessed sin brought severe judgment upon the guilty parties. Paul's encouragement to them was, "But let a man examine himself, and so let him eat of that bread, and drink of that cup" (1 Cor 11:28). The alternative would be God's discipline in the form of sickness and physical death.

Third, godly people experience sickness and suffering. Obviously, this biblical teaching is diametrically opposed to the prosperity gospel. Hank Hanegraff, in *Christianity in Crisis*, cites several examples that verify this reality.[63]

> Job, who is affirmed by Scripture as a great man of faith, was covered with painful sores from the soles of his feet to the top of his head (Job 2:7, "So went Satan forth from the presence of the LORD, and smote Job with sore boils from the sole of his foot unto his crown").
>
> The great apostle Paul confessed to the Galatian believers that because of a bodily illness, he preached the gospel to them for the first time (Gal 4:13, "Ye know how through infirmity of the flesh I preached the gospel unto you at the first").

---

[62] "For we know that the whole creation groaneth and travaileth in pain together until now. And not only they, but ourselves also, which have the first-fruits of the Spirit, even we ourselves groan within ourselves, waiting for the adoption, to wit, the redemption of our body" (Rom 8:22–23).

[63] Hank Hanegraff, *Christianity in Crisis* (Eugene, OR: Harvest House, 1993), 252–53.

Timothy, Paul's son in the faith, suffered from frequent stomach problems. Instead of telling Timothy to "positively confess" his healing, Paul gave him some practical advice. Paul told Timothy to "Drink no longer water, but use a little wine for thy stomach's sake and thine often infirmities" (1 Tim 5:23).

Elisha the prophet was blessed with a double portion of God's anointing, and yet suffered and died a sick man (2 Kgs 13:14a, "Now Elisha was fallen sick of his sickness whereof he died").

Paul left Trophimus sick in Miletus (2 Tim 4:20, "Erastus abode at Corinth: but Trophimus have I left at Miletum sick"), and Epaphroditus fell ill and nearly died (Phil 2:25–30, especially verse 27, "For indeed he was sick nigh unto death: but God had mercy on him; and not on him only, but on me also, lest I should have sorrow upon sorrow").

Fourth, God has, at times, used affliction for his glory. Again, this principle stands in contrast to the prosperity gospel. God's Word records at least two instances when this transpired. One of these instances is King David's declaration that God's chastening him was an act of covenant faithfulness. David exclaimed, "It is good for me that I have been afflicted; that I might learn thy statutes . . . I know, O LORD, that thy judgments are right, and that thou in faithfulness hast afflicted me" (Ps 119:71, 75). A second instance is in John 9, where Jesus states emphatically that a man's blindness was not the result of inherited or personal sins. Rather, his blindness, and subsequent healing, was for the glory of God. When asked by his disciples whose sin caused the man's blindness, Jesus said, "Neither hath this man sinned, nor his parents: but that the works of God should be made manifest in him" (John 9:3). The healing of the man born blind was a public display of God's glory that would not have been possible had God not allowed the man to be born blind. While Christ's atonement will lead to the healing of our bodies in heaven, Christians should agree with Hanegraff when he says, "We will continue to suffer the effects of the fall (such as sickness and disease) until God establishes a new heaven and a new earth wherein dwells righteousness."[64]

False Assumption Regarding Wealth

The idea that God desires all his children to be rich is the second false assumption of prosperity theology. If it is God's will that all Christians be rich, how does one explain the impoverished conditions of faithful believers living in third world countries? On five separate occasions it was this writer's

---

[64] Hanegraff, *Christianity in Crisis*, 252.

privilege to do missionary work in Ghana, West Africa. The Christians in Ghana were genuine in their faith, exuberant in their worship, and hungry for God's Word. And yet the vast majority of them live in abject poverty.

What is the biblical teaching on wealth? While there is inherently nothing wrong with wealth, people sin when they allow money to become an object of affection and devotion. The Bible reveals at least three dangers of pursuing money.

First, those who focus on material wealth are prone to forget the giver of their wealth. All material blessings are the result of God's mercy and grace. In Deuteronomy 8:10–14, God warned Israel about the spiritual amnesia of emphasizing blessings above him:

> When thou hast eaten and art full, then thou shalt bless the LORD thy God for the good land which he hath given thee. Beware that thou forget not the LORD thy God, in not keeping his commandments, and his judgments, and his statutes, which I command thee this day: Lest when thou hast eaten and art full, and hast built goodly houses, and welt therein; And when thy herds and thy flocks multiply, and thy silver and thy gold is multiplied, and all that thou hast is multiplied; Then thine heart be lifted up, and thou forget the LORD thy God, which brought thee forth out of the land of Egypt, from the house of bondage.

Second, the pursuit of money often stems from covetousness, which generates insensitivity toward God and others. This is what happened with the rich man in Luke 12, whose improper attitude toward material prosperity was revealed in his self-absorbed statements:

> What shall I do, because I have no room where to bestow all my fruits and my goods? And he said, This will I do: I will pull down my barns, and build greater; and there will I bestow all my fruits and my goods. And I will say to my soul, Soul, thou hast much goods laid up for many years; take thine ease, eat, drink, and be merry. (Luke 12:17–19)

But God says to him, "Thou fool, this night thy soul shall be required of thee: then whose shall those things be, which thou hast provided?" Jesus concludes the parable, "So is he that layeth up treasure for himself, and is not rich toward God" (Luke 12:20–21). The pursuit of money often stems from covetousness.

Third, the love of money leads to snares and temptations. As Paul reminded Timothy,

> But they that will be rich fall into temptation and a snare, and into many foolish and hurtful lusts, which drown men in destruction and perdition. For the love of money is the root of all evil: which while some coveted after, thy have erred from the faith, and pierce themselves through with many sorrows. (1 Tim 6:9–10)

As shoots grow out of a root, all sorts of evil things grow out of the love of money. It produces hurts, worries, pangs of conscience, and hurtful temptations which reveal an ungodly, discontent spirit. "But godliness with contentment is great gain. For we brought nothing into this world, and it is certain we can carry nothing out. And having food and raiment let us be therewith content" (1 Tim 6:6–8).

Prosperity theology makes money the top priority in life. Its preachers guarantee vast riches if their hearers will do two things: (1) believe God wants them to be rich and (2) plant seeds of faith (i.e., money) back into prosperity gospel ministries, knowing that people reap in proportion to what they sow. Why is this movement so popular in churches today? Perhaps because it feeds off society's disillusionment and desires.

Vast numbers of African Americans are disillusioned with their present economic status. Barely making ends meet, most of them want more. Prosperity theology becomes the welcomed solution to their problems. Packaged neatly with biblical catchphrases and success stories, the prosperity message is presented with excitement and enthusiasm. Like a desert mirage, this false gospel proffers life and health but only delivers to the disillusioned mouthfuls of dry, empty promises. Unfortunately, their hopes are dashed to pieces when at the end of the day their economic status hasn't changed.

SUMMATION OF THE CRISIS

An Open Attack on the Gospel

To say the gospel is under attack is an understatement. Some African American preachers have bought into Satan's plan of watering down God's truth with the social gospel, black liberation theology, and the prosperity gospel. While these men claim to be preaching the gospel of Christ, they are, in reality, preaching a different gospel. The messages projected from their pulpits are anything but the "good news." Instead they are bad news messages that keep people enslaved to their sin with no prospect of escape.

The prosperity movement is especially threatening to African American churches. By adding a health and wealth feature to their message, prosperity preachers distort God's truth and leave people in a quandary, not knowing what is meant by "gospel." Pulpits in general and African American pulpits in particular should maintain the purity and integrity of the gospel of Jesus Christ. As God's Word is correctly analyzed, explained, and applied, the preacher exalts its integrity.

Paul's admonition in Galatians 1:6–9 applies well to the contemporary African American church:

> I marvel that ye are so soon removed from him that called you into the grace of Christ unto another gospel: Which is not another; but there be some that trouble you, and would pervert the gospel of Christ. But though we, or an angel from heaven, preach any other gospel unto you than that which we have preached unto you, let him be accursed. As we said before, so say I now again, if any man preach any other gospel unto you than that ye have received, let him be accursed.

Expressing his concerns over false teachers who were troubling the Galatian Christians, Paul exposes the danger of tampering with the gospel message. This is the same situation that many African American churches currently find themselves in. How can accuracy and relevance in biblical preaching be restored to African American pulpits? What can African American churches do to maintain the purity of the gospel? Paul outlines three ways God's people can protect the integrity of Christ's gospel.

First, African American churches must acknowledge the existence of a counterfeit gospel. Paul says, "I marvel that ye are so soon removed from him that called you into the grace of Christ unto *another* gospel" (Gal 1:6, emphasis added). The Greek word translated as "another" in this verse is *heteros*, which means "another of a different kind."[65] Paul says the Judaizers were teaching a different gospel altogether. What made this different gospel so appealing was that it resembled, to some extent, the true gospel. It was presented with theological and practical terminology that enticed gullible Christians. The Galatians needed to recognize this different gospel for what it was and reject it. Likewise, the African American church must come to understand that an entirely different gospel exists today; one that is man-made, self-induced, and false.

Second, African American churches must affirm the one and only true gospel of Jesus Christ. Paul adds, "But there be some that trouble you, and

---

[65] Herman Wolfgang Beyer, *TDNT*, vol. 2, ed. G. Kittel (Grand Rapids, MI: Wm B. Eerdmans, Co, 1964), 702–4.

would pervert the gospel of Christ" (Gal 1:7). Paul refers to the gospel as the "gospel of Christ," which is the good news about Jesus Christ. It is the good news that Jesus Christ, "died for our sins, according to the scriptures; and that he was buried, and that he rose again the third day according to the scriptures" (1 Cor 15:3–4). The message presented by the agitating Judaizers in Galatia was diametrically opposed to the gospel of Christ. It had perverted, twisted, or distorted the true gospel message.

Christ himself had previously exhorted his disciples about this very truth. Is it possible there is more than one true gospel? Is it possible there are many ways of becoming a child of God? When comforting his disciples just prior to his death and resurrection, Jesus said, "I am the way, the truth and the life: no man cometh unto the Father but by me" (John 14:6). There is only one way to God the Father, and that is through his Son, Jesus Christ. There exists but one true gospel.

Third, African American churches must declare that God judges those who distort his Word. Paul further states, "But though we, or an angel from heaven, preach any other gospel unto you than that which we have preached unto you, let him be accursed" (Gal 1:8). Paul is not asserting that he or an angel is likely to preach heresy. Rather, he uses a hypothetical possibility to illustrate his point. An "anathema" is pronounced on anyone who preaches a false gospel. That means false preachers will be turned over to God as accursed objects and judged accordingly. Any preacher who manipulates the gospel of Christ by altering or misinterpreting it will be severely disciplined by God. This serves as a warning to all who have been commissioned by God to communicate his Word.

The Seriousness of Mishandling God's Word

Jeremiah's warning to Israel underscores the seriousness of mishandling God's Word. In Jeremiah 23, the prophet goes to great lengths to warn Israel while also rebuking the pseudo-prophets. Jeremiah's warnings about Israel's impending doom were met with mockery from the false prophets who had replaced Jeremiah's message of warning with their own words of peace.[66] God intervened by giving Jeremiah words of reproof to communicate to the lying prophets. If these lying prophets had only listened to God's Word, they would have known Israel's judgment was inescapable. Instead, they altered and exploited God's Word. God said of these lying prophets,

---

[66] See Jer 6:13–14; 8:10–11; 14:14–16; 28:1–4, 10–11; 29:8–9, 20–23, 31–32.

> And I have seen folly in the prophets of Samaria; they prophesied in Baal, and caused my people Israel to err. I have seen also in the prophets of Jerusalem an horrible thing: they commit adultery, and walk in lies: they strengthen also the hands of evildoers, that none doth return from his wickedness: they are full of them unto me as Sodom, and the inhabitants thereof as Gomorrah. . . . Thus saith the LORD of hosts, Hearken not unto the words of the prophets that prophesy unto you: they make you vain: they speak a vision of their own hearty, and not out of the mouth of the LORD. They say still unto them that despise me, the LORD hath said, Ye shall have peace. . . . I have not sent these prophets, yet they ran: I have not spoken to them, yet they prophesied.[67]

God exposed the lying prophets for what they really were: charlatans, rip-off artists, deceivers, peddlers of lies. They spoke without being appointed by God. Their message was not God's words but words they had invented themselves. They claimed God had given them their message, but in reality their words had no substance to them or power behind them. As a consequence, God said,

> Is not my word like as a fire? saith the LORD: and like a hammer that breaketh the rock in pieces? Therefore, behold, I am against the prophets, saith the LORD, that steal my words every man from his neighbor. Behold, I am against the prophets, saith the LORD, that use their tongues, and say, He saith. Behold, I am against them that prophesy false dreams, saith the LORD, and do tell them, and cause my people to err by their lies, and by their lightness; yet I sent them not, nor commanded them: therefore they shall not profit this people at all, saith the LORD.[68]

The messages expounded by the false prophets resulted in the spiritual downfall of the nation. As a result of listening to lies, the people's spiritual and moral standards were lowered. Further, they misunderstood the nature of God, living under the false assumption that he would never allow them to be overwhelmed by their enemies. Instead of encouraging the people to love, honor, and obey God, the false prophets incited rebellion. African American churches would do well to heed Jeremiah's warning and reject false preachers of the social gospel, black liberation theology, and the prosperity gospel. If they don't, black congregations, like Israel before them, may experience God's discipline.

---

[67] Jeremiah 23:13–14, 16–17a, 21.
[68] Jeremiah 23:29–32.

DISCUSSION QUESTIONS

1. Have you or any member of your family ever experienced racial discrimination? If so, explain.
2. What are your thoughts regarding racism in America? Does it even exist?
3. List and explain four problems created by racial segregation.
4. What is the basic premise of black liberation theology?
5. List and explain some problems associated with "black liberation theology."
6. Are there any benefits to having segregated churches or worship experiences? If so, what are they?
7. How is Psalm 139 an excellent resource for cultivating a biblical view of race?
8. How does biblically accurate and relevant preaching contribute to proper race relations in the body of Christ?
9. What are some false assumptions of prosperity theology?
10. How can local churches guard against mishandling God's Word?

2

The Importance of Biblical Exegesis

for Textual Accuracy and Relevance in Biblical Preaching

There are people among us today, teaching in our academic institutions, laboring in our denominations, pastoring in our churches, who have not departed all that far from classic biblical doctrine. They still believe that Jesus is God. They still believe in the bodily resurrection of Christ. They still believe in the virgin birth. But they do not believe that everything in Scripture is necessarily accurate and without error. They have started over the edge.[1]

ONE challenge facing the church today is that some evangelical preachers do not believe the Bible is God's final authority to man. God's Word is being manipulated by preachers who have moved away from the historic position on the nature of the Bible.[2] Is it likely that historic Christianity's epistemology is wrong and the Bible is not authoritative, or is at best one of many authorities? Of course not!

Why is biblical exegesis so important? It lays a foundation upon which truth can be determined. This chapter's focus will be on revealing exegesis's importance by defining it concisely. The debate over whether a text has a single

---

[1] Draper and Keathley, *Biblical Authority*, 1.
[2] Ibid.

meaning or multiple meanings will be introduced, and the building blocks
needed for sound exegetical study will be explained. Finally, some results of
faulty exegesis will be noted.

A DEFINITION OF EXEGESIS

The term "exegesis" is derived from the Greek word *exegeomai*, which
means, "to lead out," "to make known," or "to declare."[3] Exegesis is the thorough investigation of a biblical text in order to make known the Holy Spirit's
original intended meaning. Harold Bryson in *Expository Preaching* says the
root meaning of *exegeomai* is to "bring out the meaning of the text."[4] And Roy
B. Zuck defines exegesis as, "the determination of the meaning of the biblical
text in its historical and literary contexts."[5]

In exegesis the Bible expositor seeks to bridge the gap between the ancient
biblical text and the contemporary situation. His desire is to adequately repre-
sent what the Bible says by leading out the right meaning of the text. John 1:18
perfectly illustrates this concept. Regarding the uniqueness of Jesus Christ,
John says, "No man hath seen God at any time; the only begotten Son, which
is in the bosom of the Father, he hath declared [*exegeomai*] him." This verse
teaches that no one has ever viewed the invisible God in his full essence. This
might appear somewhat contradictory in light of what the Bible says of the
prophet Isaiah. During his vision of the heavenly throne, the prophet says he
saw "the King, the LORD of hosts" (Isa 6:5). Does this contradict John 1?
Certainly not! Most will probably agree with scholars John Walvoord and Roy
Zuck, who propose that "God may be seen in a theophany or anthropomor-
phism but His inner essence or nature is disclosed only in Jesus."[6]

No man has ever seen God in his inner essence. Jesus however, God's one
and only Son, has "exegeted" him. Jesus opens up, explains, and leads out the
meaning of God the Father to mankind. Through his person and work, Jesus
Christ fully displays the truth about the invisible God. People are able to know
what God the Father is like when they thoroughly study God the Son. Simi-
larly, people are able to know the full truth of God's Word when it is drawn
out correctly. This is biblical exegesis in its truest sense. This is what every

---

[3] W. E. Vine, *Vine's Complete Expository Dictionary of Old and New Testament Words*
(Nashville, TN: Thomas Nelson, 1996), 152.

[4] Harold T. Bryson, *Expository Preaching: The Art of Preaching Through a Book of the Bible*
(Nashville, TN: Broadman & Holman, 1995), 142.

[5] Roy B. Zuck, *Basic Bible Interpretation: A Practical Guide to Discovering Biblical Truth*
(Grand Rapids, MI: Victor, 1991), 19.

[6] John F. Walvoord and Roy B. Zuck, *The Bible Knowledge Commentary: New Testament*
(Colorado Springs, CO: David C. Cook, 1983), 273.

preacher of God's Word should seek to do. His ultimate goal should be to make known from a biblical text the author's intended meaning.

Exegesis is the opposite of reading into the biblical text one's own biases or presuppositions. Many contemporary preachers find it rewarding to read into the biblical text their personal feelings, prejudices, and opinions. An example is James Cone, who equates sound biblical preaching with black liberation theology. He argues: "Christian theology must become black theology, a theology that is unreservedly identified with the goals of the oppressed and seeks to interpret the divine character of their struggle for liberation."[7] For Cone and many of his colleagues, biblical exegesis centers on the struggle of black people for liberation. Their prejudices and biases affect their understanding of the Holy Spirit's intended meaning. True exegesis seeks to lead out of the text exactly what the Holy Spirit means to convey. Gordon Fee says, "Exegesis answers the question, what did the biblical author mean? The key to good exegesis is the ability to ask the right question in order to get the author's intended meaning."[8]

THE IMPORTANCE OF EXEGESIS

The use of exegesis in biblical preaching is predicated upon two fundamental assumptions. The first assumption is that thoughts can be accurately conveyed in words. The second assumption is that the biblical content is of such importance to mankind as to warrant the effort to discover exactly what it means. The focus of the preacher is to explain as clearly as possible what the original writer meant when he wrote the text.

The importance of exegesis to biblical preaching is further grasped by considering New Testament teaching about Scripture and the nature of the pastoral calling. For example, 2 Timothy, written from Paul's death row prison cell in Rome, admonishes Timothy to be faithful to his calling as a pastor. Timothy's primary duty as a pastor was to guard the truth of God against false teaching, according to 2 Timothy. To do this Timothy was to become an exegete, that is, one who knew how to study and accurately explain God's Word. Indeed, Paul gives three reasons why exegesis is important to biblical preaching.

---

[7] James H. Cone, *A Black Theology of Liberation* (Maryknoll, NY: Orbis, 1990), xi.

[8] Gordon D. Fee, *New Testament Exegesis* (Louisville, KY: Westminster John Knox, 1983), 31.

The Uniqueness of the Bible

First, the Bible's uniqueness necessitates exegesis. The Bible is of divine origin. Paul tells Timothy that "all scripture is given by inspiration of God" (2 Tim 3:16). The Bible is authoritative and unlike any other book. Other books may encourage and enlighten their readers; but only the Bible pierces the core of its readers' souls. The Bible is the voice of God speaking directly to human hearts. Other religions of the world base their tenets on their founders' writings. Mormons, for example, have the *Book of Mormon*, the Jehovah's Witnesses have the *New World Translation of the Holy Scriptures*, and Muslims have the Quran. The authority behind each of these writings is derived from some form of mystical experience, whereas the authority of the Bible is derived from the verbal plenary inspiration of God.

The Bible provides internal evidence of its own authenticity. When referring to Scripture as God's inspired Word, Paul says God "breathed" it by his breath or Spirit.[9] Every word in the Bible comes from the mouth of God. The word "Scripture" is the Greek word *graphe*, and means "that which is written—words, phrases, sentences (not just ideas)."[10] Inspiration is the process by which God chose to give mankind his Word. Since only the Old Testament was complete at the time Paul wrote 2 Timothy, he was obviously referring to it, but, as Kent suggests, "the qualitative emphasis leaves room for the New Testament to be considered by later Christians as within the scope of this assertion."[11]

To corroborate the inspiration of the Bible and reveal the method by which God gave mankind his Word, the apostle Peter adds:

> We have also a more sure word of prophecy; whereunto ye do well that ye take heed, as unto a light that shineth in a dark place, until the day dawn, and the day star arise in your hearts: Knowing this first that no prophecy of the scripture is of any private interpretation. For the prophecy came not in old time by the will of man: but holy men of God spake as they were moved by the Holy Ghost. (2 Pet 1:19–21)

Peter is describing God's method of giving mankind his revealed Word. God used holy men to record his truth. These men are said to have been "moved

---

[9] Homer Kent, *The Pastoral Epistles: Studies in I and II Timothy and Titus* (Chicago, IL: Moody, 1958), 209.

[10] Ibid., 290.

[11] Ibid.

by the Holy Ghost." The general idea behind this phrase is that God used his Spirit to guide the men as they wrote, guarding each and every word.

The Bible is unique in that it is authoritative. It is the very breath of God written by holy men who were guided and guarded by God's Spirit. The Spirit of God rested on and in these human instruments and spoke through them so their words did not come from themselves but from the mouth of the Living God. This is what is meant by verbal plenary inspiration. As Thiessen points out, "Thus, we speak of plenary and verbal inspiration of the Scriptures; plenary, because the inspiration is entire and without restriction, that is, it includes all and every Scripture; verbal, because it includes every word."[12]

David Walls and Max Anders add a noteworthy perspective:

> The Old Testament writers did not invent or make up their material. The Old Testament prophets were the communicators, in written form, of God's message. *Carried along* was used of a sailing ship carried along by the wind. The metaphor pictures the cooperation of the Holy Spirit with the individual writer. The prophets raised their sails, and the Holy Spirit filled them and carried their craft along in the direction he wished. Through their own unique personalities, styles of writing, and vocabularies, God moved each of them by his Spirit to communicate his truth.[13]

The Command of God

The second reason exegesis is important in biblical preaching is that God commands it. While awaiting the executioner's axe, Paul charged Timothy to "study to shew thyself approved unto God, a workman that needeth not to be ashamed, rightly dividing the word of truth" (2 Tim 2:15). This served as Timothy's call to action. As a workman for God and pastor of a local church, Timothy was instructed to correctly handle God's Word.

Because some preachers had no shame and what others were saying put them to shame, Timothy was urged to preach God's Word unashamedly. To accomplish this, Timothy needed to exegete God's Word correctly. The words "rightly divide" translate the Greek word *orthotomeo*, which is derived from two words, *orthos*, meaning "straight," and *temno*, meaning "to cut."[14] Paul

---

[12] Henry C. Thiessen, *Lectures in Systematic Theology*, revised by Vernon D. Doerksen (Grand Rapids, MI: Wm. B. Eerdmans, 1979), 65.

[13] David Walls and Max Anders, *1 & 2 Peter, 1, 2, & 3 John, Jude*, Holman New Testament Commentary (Nashville, TN: Broadman & Holman, 1999), 114.

[14] Vine, *Vine's Complete Expository Dictionary of Old and New Testament Words*, 178.

tells Timothy to cut straight the Word of God.[15] He was to handle God's Word honestly, fully, and straightforwardly, plowing a straight furrow in exploring and expounding the Scriptures.[16] John Phillips comments:

> To divide the word of truth rightly, we must have a consistent her-
> meneutic. We must interpret the Bible not allegorically but literally,
> taking into account the Hebrew and Greek languages of its birth
> and making allowances for the cultural, historical, and geographical
> backgrounds against which it arose. . . . If we follow these guide-
> lines, an adequate, comprehensive, consistent, and correct exegesis
> of the text should emerge from our study.[17]

God commands preachers to carefully exegete his Word. Their goal should be to become unashamed workers, who, through diligent and careful study of the Scriptures, can "rightly divide" its truths to others. It is every preacher's duty to cut straight the Word of God.

The Rejection of the Truth

Third, exegesis is important to biblical preaching because of the wide-spread rejection of God's truth. As evidenced in Paul's charge to Timothy, even Christians have a propensity to reject the truth of God's Word. Paul's charge to "preach the word" (2 Tim 4:2) was intended to counter heresies that would divert God's people from the truth.

Motivated by their own sinful desires, the people of Timothy's day had developed an ear for preaching that communicated what they wanted to hear as opposed to what they needed to hear. Such preaching would turn the people of God away from the truth. When that occurred, people would begin the process of accumulating to themselves teachers who would feed their fleshly desires. The end result would be disastrous. They would eventually refuse to listen to the truth altogether.[18] Paul forewarned Timothy about this: "For the time will come when they will not endure sound doctrine; but after their own lusts shall they heap to themselves teachers, having itching ears; And they shall turn away their ears from the truth, and shall be turned unto fables" (2 Tim 4:3–4).

Sound biblical exegesis is important when one considers the spiri-tual climate of our culture. People crave preaching that coincides with their

---

[15] Kent, *The Pastoral Epistles*, 274.

[16] John Phillips, *Exploring the Pastoral Epistles: An Expository Commentary* (Grand Rapids, MI: Kregel, 2004), 381.

[17] Ibid.

[18] Kent, *The Pastoral Epistles*, 294.

flesh-driven lifestyles. Many so-called Christ followers display little interest in hearing the truth about God, sin, Jesus Christ, heaven, hell, or themselves. Perhaps some preachers, for fear of losing hearers, money, or even popularity, dilute God's Word and adopt a more accepting, "user-friendly" approach to preaching. Such an approach accommodates sinful lifestyles and majors on emotionalism while leaving listeners spiritually dazed and confused.

EXEGETICAL CRISIS: SINGLE VERSUS MULTIPLE MEANINGS

One factor precipitating this dearth of biblical preaching is a refusal among preachers to draw out of the text the Spirit of God's one intended meaning for the original readers. Walter Kaiser calls this the "current crisis in exegetical theology."[19] The crisis centers on how preachers relate "what the text meant in its historical context, to what the same text means in the present context."[20]

Some Bible scholars find it unreasonable to expect that God would give one meaning to a biblical text. Should we not expect several meanings given the diversity of cultures, backgrounds, and situations among the original authors and readers? Add to this the reality that times have changed since the writing of the Bible and word meanings have changed over time. It hardly seems reasonable to assume God sought to communicate just one meaning from each biblical passage . . . or does it?

Such questions have merit. In response, we must clarify what is meant by the assertion that each biblical text has only one meaning. First, we're not denying that a biblical text can have many different implications and various applications for individual readers. Neither are we denying that the Holy Spirit can use a single passage to spur different readers to take different actions. We are asserting that the original, God-inspired authors of Scripture intended to communicate a single meaning to their original audience.

For many the issue is whether a given text's meaning is determined by the author or the reader.[21] Most conservative preachers espouse the former view. Assuming meaning is generated by the author, Keith Willhite argues, "is the best way to preach, or at least, to learn to preach."[22] Willhite's premise is that having a high view of Scripture will force preachers to take a text-centered approach to their study and preaching. Willhite rightly says, "Though a text

---

[19] Walter C. Kaiser Jr., *Toward an Exegetical Theology: Biblical Exegesis for Preaching & Teaching* (Grand Rapids, MI: Baker, 1981), 23.

[20] Ibid.

[21] Ibid., 24.

[22] Keith Willhite and Scott M. Gibson, *The Big Idea of Biblical Preaching* (Grand Rapids, MI: Baker, 1998), 14.

may say many things, listeners need to hear the synthesis of what was intended."[23] By synthesis is meant the exegetical idea, the original meaning, the single sense of the text.

Liberal theologians like William A. Beardslee, Charles Mabee, and Ronald L. Farmer hold to a "process hermeneutic," which argues for varied or multiple meanings to any Scripture text.[24] According to process hermeneutics, the meaning of the text is "open-ended," taking specific form only insofar as the reader makes a contribution to it.[25] This suggests the intended meaning of a text is determined more by the reader than the author.

Robert L. Thomas, in his book *Evangelical Hermeneutics*, compares traditional grammatical-historical interpretation with the new evangelical hermeneutic. He rightly notes,

> That a single passage has one meaning and one meaning only has been a long-established principle of biblical interpretation. Among evangelicals, recent violations of that principle have multiplied . . . the single meaning principle is of foundational importance in our understanding of God's communication with humankind, just as it has been since the creation of the human race. The entrance of sin in Genesis 3 brought confusion to our communication with God that has continued ever since.[26]

Thomas critiques those who intimate the possibility of a text's having "related sub-meanings,"[27] a perspective that enables theologians to acknowledge traditional hermeneutics while seeking sub-meanings within the meaning. Thomas additionally argues that God has communicated with humans using the single meaning method from the beginning of time.

> Someone needs to sound the alarm when evangelical leaders mislead the body of Christ. A mass evangelical exodus from the time-honored principle of interpreting Scripture is jeopardizing the church's access to the truths taught therein. Whether the interpreters have forsaken the principle intentionally or have subconsciously ignored it, the damage is the same. The only hope of escape from the pit into which so many have fallen is to reaffirm the principle of single

---

[23] Ibid., 22.
[24] Ronald L. Farmer, *Beyond the Impasse: The Promise of a Process Hermeneutic* (Atlanta, GA: Mercer University Press, 1977).
[25] Ibid., 121.
[26] Robert L. Thomas, *Evangelical Hermeneutics: The New Versus the Old* (Grand Rapids, MI: Kregel, 2002), 141.
[27] Ibid., 157.

meaning, along with the other hermeneutical principles that have served the believing community so well through the centuries.[28]

For conservative preachers, biblical exegesis seeks to determine the single idea of the text. It realizes that the text may say many things but there is only one intended meaning.

BUILDING BLOCKS TO SOUND EXEGESIS

Sound exegesis is contingent upon several ministerial disciplines. Although the preacher may have had good courses in exegesis that covered syntax, textual criticism, and Greek and Hebrew vocabulary, he will still face a struggle each time he prepares to preach. He realizes, as Thomas concludes, that, "Bible exposition includes much more than exegesis. In a logical development of theological and ministerial disciplines, it is built upon other fields of investigation as well."[29]

While biblical theology, church history, apologetics, and homiletics can all contribute to exegesis, Thomas concludes that the disciplines most crucial to sound exegesis include: Bible introduction, biblical languages, and hermeneutics.[30] The following will summarize those disciplines and how they contribute to the exegetical task.

Biblical Introduction

Biblical introduction covers the subjects of inspiration, canonicity, authority, and answers the significant questions: How did we get our Bible? Who wrote the Bible? Why do we believe the Bible? Without a proper understanding of such concepts, the preacher's Bible study and interpretation methods will be suspect. He will be more likely to believe the Bible is a purely human document and therefore contains errors and/or contradictions.

Biblical Languages

This discipline deals with syntax, grammar, and vocabulary and seeks to discover the original meaning Old Testament Hebrew and New Testament Greek texts. Studying biblical languages includes learning the basic grammatical structure of the original languages, their alphabets, pronunciation, and

---

[28] Ibid., 160.

[29] Robert L. Thomas, "Exegesis and Expository Preaching," in *Rediscovering Expository Preaching*, ed. Richard Mayhue (Dallas: Word, 1992), 143.

[30] Ibid., 143–47.

vocabulary. It also includes learning to rightly use study tools such as dictionaries, concordances, lexicons, and commentaries.

Hermeneutics

Hermeneutics seeks to provide principles for accurately interpreting the Bible. The word "hermeneutics" is of Greek origin from the word *hermeneou*, meaning "to interpret" or "to make plain." Hermeneutics gives the preacher solid principles from which to discover the original writer's intended meaning.

Personal Observation. Biblical exegesis is crucial in obtaining an accurate understanding of God's Word. It will help to determine the correct meaning of a given text. Without determining the correct meaning, the sermon application will be inaccurate. The exegetical methodology of the preacher determines whether he is cutting straight God's Word of truth or reading into it his own presuppositions. Erroneous methodology has led to the propagation of three erroneous belief systems: the social gospel, black liberation theology, and prosperity theology. Much of their theological premise is based on the erroneous assumption that the meaning of a Bible text is determined by the reader. This is extremely dangerous and has contributed to relativism, misplaced priorities, gospel confusion, and inappropriate forms of church leadership. These phenomena collectively have contributed to a large number of spiritually impotent African American churches.

Faulty Exegesis Leads to Relativism. The first result of faulty exegesis is relativism. The goal of exegesis is to discover the original author's intent. Anything less creates an atmosphere where truth is regarded as relative. It is to be expected that the unregenerate might question or even reject the truth. The Bible teaches that biblical truth is "spiritually discerned" (1 Cor 2:14), and therefore only those who possess the Spirit of God can fully grasp and understand it. Yet even in many contemporary religious settings, God's truth is no longer regarded as absolute. Truth, we are told, is relative, based on circumstances and situations. What is true today may be false tomorrow. What is truth to one may not be truth to another.

Relativism has contributed to the moral collapse of our nation in general and of the body of Christ in particular. While the body of Christ is experiencing many moral ills within its ranks, two are more prevalent than others: homosexuality and abortion. When relativism replaces biblical absolutes, homosexuality and abortion are easily justified.

African American pulpits must sound the alarm against these evil practices while imploring people to accept God's love and mercy offered through his

Son, Jesus Christ. No longer should the black church allow practicing homosexuals to lead worship and preach. To do so gives the erroneous impression that God has exception clauses for those in service to him.

Faulty Exegesis Leads to Misplaced Priorities. The second result of faulty exegesis is misplaced priorities. Our African American communities are inundated with heresy regarding the gospel of Jesus Christ. Many preachers have adopted the so-called "Full Gospel" mind-set and have consequently found an open platform on cable television to promote their heresy. The true gospel is being distorted today because a wealth feature has been added to it. Perpetrators of error preach supposedly good news about prosperity, as opposed to good news about the Lord Jesus Christ.

Prosperity theology supporters maintain it is God's will that every Christian be financially wealthy. To be blessed with financial wealth, people are required to sow financial seeds to the preachers and ministries that support this idea. This idea finds fertile soil in the hearts of those dominated by covetousness, who will flock to churches where financial prosperity is the focus. Such people will at times sacrifice their last dollar, giving it away to preachers or their ministries.

Prosperity theology maintains that the Bible validates its claims in at least two passages. The first is Galatians 3:14: "That the blessing of Abraham might come on the Gentiles through Jesus Christ; that we might receive the promise of the Spirit through faith." Christians are entitled to all the blessings of Abraham through faith, prosperity preachers assert, noting that Abraham was very rich.[31] Therefore, Christians should possess houses, land, and inheritances as descendants of Abraham through faith.[32]

Prosperity gospel preachers fail to realize, however, that the text is making reference to the blessing of a spiritual heritage. Its emphasis is not material blessings.[33] Paul states that the blessing we receive is the indwelling presence and power of the Spirit of God, whom we receive the very moment we put our faith in Jesus Christ. To be in possession of the Spirit of God far surpasses being in possession of wealth.

The second passage supposedly endorsing the prosperity gospel is Luke 6:38: "Give, and it shall be given to you; good measure, pressed down, and shaken together, and running over, shall men give into your bosom. For with the same measure that ye mete withal it shall be measured to you again."

---

[31] "And Abram was very rich in cattle, silver, and in gold" (Gen 13:2).
[32] Bowens, *Prosperity Gospel*, 55.
[33] Ibid.

A careful analysis of this verse and its immediate context discloses its intended meaning. The Lord Jesus Christ had just finished pronouncing woes on those whose misplaced priorities had caused them to reject him in favor of pursuing riches and popularity. Jesus said,

> But woe unto you that are rich! for ye have received your consolation. Woe unto you that are full! for ye shall hunger. Woe unto you that laugh now! for ye shall mourn and weep. Woe unto you, when all men shall speak well of you! for so did their fathers to the false prophets. (Luke 6:24–26)

In contrast to the selfish attitudes of the people, Jesus instructs his disciples on the subject of unconditional love, reminding them true love is active and never passive, performed supernaturally through the enabling of God's Spirit. True love is exhibited from the principle that Christ's followers will treat others the way they want to be treated (Luke 6:31).

The overall emphasis of the passage is love and how to treat others caringly. Jesus's teaching is geared more toward spiritual concerns than physical concerns. While it is true that God sometimes blesses those who are financially generous with more wealth, this discourse focused on the spiritual blessings received by those who exhibit kindness to others. No believer in Christ will ever be considered a loser if he performs self-denying, self-sacrificing actions.

When a preacher concludes this passage guarantees financial success, he is revealing a faulty exegetical approach. He more than likely resorts to a "proof-text" method of Bible study. Commenting on the dangers of this method, Walter Kaiser and Moises Silva note,

> The proof-text method often relies on a naïve reading of the text. It may disregard the purpose for which the text was written, the historical conditioning in which it is set, and the genre conventions that shaped it. Consequently, this method is vulnerable to allegorization, psychologization, spiritualization, and other forms of quick-and-easy adjustments of the scriptural words to say what one wishes them to say in the contemporary scene, ignoring the intended purpose and usage as determined by content, grammar, and historical background.[34]

African American preachers must encourage their congregants to trust God rather than pursue wealth. In and of itself wealth is not sinful. It is not wrong to have money, or an abundance of it. Sin occurs when a person places

---

[34] Walter C. Kaiser and Moises Silva, *An Introduction to Biblical Hermeneutics: The Search for Meaning* (Grand Rapids, MI: Zondervan, 1994), 31–32.

wealth above commitment to God. Instead of preaching about financial success, the preaching time would be better served by instructing people to seek God.

In a portion of the Sermon on the Mount, Jesus did precisely this, encouraging his listeners to trust God and not focus on material possessions. He warned them of the dangers of misplaced priorities, which can generate anxiety:

> No man can serve two masters: for either he will hate the one, and love the other; or else he will hold to the one, and despise the other. Ye cannot serve God and mammon. Therefore I say unto you, Take no thought for your life, what ye shall eat, or what ye shall drink; nor yet for your body, what ye shall put on. Is not the life more than meat, and the body than raiment? . . . Therefore take no thought, saying, What shall we eat? Or, What shall we drink? Or, Wherewithal shall we be clothed? (For after all these things do the Gentiles seek) for your heavenly Father knoweth that ye have need of these things. But seek ye first the kingdom of God, and his righteousness; and all these things shall be added unto you. (Matt 6:24–25, 31–33)

Jesus urged his followers to develop a spiritual philosophy of life which wards off materialism and worry. He said a person's life should not be measured in terms of the physical. Yet Jesus did not forbid the possession of wealth or material goods. Rather, he said they have no permanent or abiding quality.

If the Christian is not to be preoccupied with accumulating wealth or anxiety over the basic needs of life, what should his concern be? What should be the Christian's priority in life? The answer is God's kingdom and God's righteousness (Matt 6:33). God's kingdom means his sovereign rule in heaven and on earth; most especially in the life of the Christian. To seek God's kingdom is to seek to ensure that his righteousness is done in heaven, on earth, and in and through the life of the Christian.[35]

Faulty Exegesis Leads to Gospel Confusion. The third result of faulty exegesis is gospel confusion. Exegesis means drawing out of the Bible its exact meaning. Eisegesis means reading into the text one's personal bias and suppositions. The unfortunate prevalence of eisegesis in preaching today has bolstered many false beliefs.

While there is much merit to emphasizing the practical side of Christianity, preachers must stand guard against obscuring the message of Jesus Christ

---

[35] Stuart K. Weber, *Matthew*, Holman New Testament Commentary (Nashville, TN: Broadman & Holman, 2000), 88.

with a purely social gospel. When the true gospel message is obscured by social and economic concerns, people can be misled.

African American preachers must be given to sound exegesis and devote themselves to explaining that Jesus Christ's death, burial, and resurrection is the true gospel message (see 1 Cor 15:1–4). Anything short of explaining that truth is tantamount to preaching heresy.

Faulty Exegesis Leads to Inappropriate Church Leadership. The final result of faulty exegesis is that it has led to unbiblical models of church leadership. Specifically, some African American churches have placed women in leadership positions that are limited to men, as qualified by Scripture. This problem crosses denominational lines, with Baptist, Pentecostal, Methodist, and non-denominational churches instituting female pastoral leadership.

In his book *The Prophethood of Black Believers*, J. Deotis Roberts grounds his endorsement of female pastors and preachers in "black theological reflection." He writes:

> Against the background of black theological reflection we have asserted the unqualified right of women to practice ministry in the church of Jesus Christ. Those who fence the pulpit and ban women from it have asserted an authority that they do not have. It is God alone who calls humans, male and female, to minister in his redemptive cause. . . . There are no Christian biblical or theological grounds that would prohibit anyone, called and commissioned by God to minister, from practicing fully the divine summons as servant and minister in the name of Jesus Christ. It is now inevitable that women of all races will act as ordained ministers of the church. It behooves male pastors to prepare the way for God's will to be done. The role of women in the black church is crucial for its survival and effectiveness. It is clear that that status of black women will soon be upgraded by male leadership or by women themselves. The rationale for keeping women out of the pulpit or in subordinate positions will not be long accepted.[36]

What exactly does God's Word teach about female pastors and preachers? Paul's letters to Timothy shed much light on the subject. In these letters, he is deeply concerned that church members know how to behave according to biblical criteria. In demonstrating what proper behavior looks like, Paul discusses qualifications for pastors and deacons. Among the points he makes clear is that the office of pastor-teacher is limited to males. Paul states emphatically, "This

---

[36] J. Deotis Roberts, *The Prophethood of Black Believers: An African-American Political Theology for Ministry* (Louisville, KY: Westminster John Knox, 1994), 87–88.

is a true saying, if a man desire the office of a bishop, he desireth a good work" (1 Tim 3:1).

The Spirit of God is conveying the truth that only males should serve in the leadership capacity of pastor, referenced here by the term "bishop." The word for "man" in this verse is not the generic term *anthropos*, which can refer to humankind in general without gender distinction. The word used is *tis* denoting "any person."[37] Who does "any person" refer to? The meaning is explained in the next verse. Paul says the one desiring the pastorate must be the "husband of one wife" (1 Tim 3:2). The word "husband" is the Greek word, *aner*,[38] denoting one of masculine gender.

Paul was acutely aware that women as well as men had spiritual giftedness and should serve Christ. However, proper textual analysis yields evidence that Paul was expecting pastors to all be males. Only a man can be the "husband of one wife," and thus only a man is qualified to serve as pastor. This signifies that men and women, equally justified in Christ, played complementary rather than identical roles in the early church.

While every Christian regardless of gender has been gifted by God to serve the church, only males have been called to serve as its pastor-teachers. And while every Christian is commissioned by God to "Go ye into all the world, and preach the gospel" (Mark 16:15), not every Christian has been duly called by God to publicly preach his Word in the context of the church's gathered worship.

In many African American churches, women are being ordained to serve as pastors. The biblical text normally cited to justify this is found in the book of Joel where the prophet exclaims, "And it shall come to pass afterward, that I will pour out my spirit upon all flesh; and your sons and daughters shall prophesy, your old men shall dream dreams, your young men shall see visions" (Joel 2:28). Advocates for female pastors interpret this verse to mean God is raising a generation of women ("your daughters") who have been assigned the task of preaching his Word as pastors during the worship of local churches. They have taken this verse completely out of its context.

---

[37] Robert G. Gromacki, *Stand True to the Charge: An Exposition of 1 Timothy* (Schaumburg, IL: Regular Baptist Press, 1982), 75.

[38] The word *aner* occurs 216 times in the New Testament. It is a strongly male-marked term, in contrast to *anthropos*, which can mean either "man" or "person." There are several other examples in the New Testament where this word is used to eliminate the gender-neutral hypothesis. Examples can be found in Chapter 6 of Vern S. Poythress and Wayne A. Grudem, *The Gender-Neutral Bible Controversy: Muting the Masculinity of God's Word* (Nashville, TN: Broadman & Holman, 2000), 101–9.

The immediate context makes reference to the advent of divine blessings and the outpouring of God's Spirit on Israel. This event was partially fulfilled on the Day of Pentecost when the apostle Peter quoted this prophecy in response to an inquiry about the phenomenon of speaking in tongues (see Acts 2:16–21). Its ultimate realization however, is yet to come. As Walvoord and Zuck note,

> The context indicates that "all people" refers specifically to all inhabitants of Judah (cf. the threefold use of *your* in v. 28, as well as the parallel passages in Ezekiel 39:29 and Zechariah 12:10). This will be true regardless of age, gender, or social class. At that time recipients of the divine Spirit will exercise prophetic gifts which in the past had been limited to a select few (cf. 1 Samuel 10:10–11; 19:20–24).[39]

The phrase, "at that time," is closely connected with the events following the rapture of the church, the glorious return of Jesus Christ, and his subsequent Kingdom rule. Midway through the tribulation period a great spiritual revival will take place on earth. When a fresh outpouring of God's Spirit falls on 144,000 witnesses, they will go about preaching the gospel. As a result multitudes will be saved.[40]

By spiritualizing or reading personal opinions into the biblical text, advocates of female pastors compromise God's truth, as evidenced by an influx of women being ordained into pastoral ministries in urban churches. This situation has contributed to a deep-seated problem for African American families. Indeed, the African American family is imperiled by what many believe to be the "feminization" of our society as a whole. With almost two-thirds of African American homes being run by females, having women serve as pastors only increases the odds that boys will grow up with gender role confusion. As boys mature to manhood, the biblical instruction on submission is blurred by what they see in their pulpits.

Regardless of a church's size, ministry impact, or voluminous budget, if it has women pastors, it has distorted God's Word. Sound biblical exegesis safeguards the church against such a tragedy.

---

[39] John F. Walvoord and Roy B. Zuck, eds., *The Bible Knowledge Commentary: Old Testament* (Colorado Springs, CO: David C. Cook, 1985), 1420.

[40] John Phillips, *Exploring the Minor Prophets: An Expository Commentary* (Grand Rapids, MI: Kregel, 1998), 78.

More Negative Results of Faulty Exegesis

Biblical exegesis is necessary for accurately explaining and applying God's Word of truth, and sadly this differs greatly from the approach of many contemporary preachers. Many read their personal biases and presuppositions into the biblical text as opposed to allowing the text to speak for itself. For example, Yale theologian David Kelsey says, "[The fact that] faith communities interpret Scripture in different ways supports my discovery of a distinctly black construal of Scripture . . . there is no single normative understanding of Scripture to which all must subscribe . . . different theologians see different patterns in Scripture."[41] As an African American student of the Bible, this writer finds Kelsey's statement appalling. The predominantly black church in America is in the spiritually depleted state it is in due to statements like this. It appears the racial dynamic in America has resulted in two opposing worldviews. The worldview adopted by many white Americans is one of racial superiority while many black Americans focus on survival, equality, and liberation. As a consequence, some African American preachers study, interpret, and preach God's Word through the lens of what Cone termed, "a black theology of liberation."[42] Such theology is one that identifies with the goals of the oppressed and seeks to interpret the divine character of their struggle for liberation.

Another example of reading personal bias into the biblical text is Ronald L. Farmer. He believes there is an "evolutionary nature"[43] of the text. By this Farmer means the text is always the partial, inexact expression of the author's real propositions. Farmer calls the biblical text "proposals of propositions,"[44] in total agreement with Alfred North Whitehead. Both are of the conviction that, "If the Scriptural text inevitably evoke[s] new propositions during the course of time, what the text might come to mean can theoretically be more important than anything the text has meant in the past."[45] This suggests the original author's intended meaning is of little consequence for today's contemporary audience. In fact, the preacher can essentially decide for himself what he senses the text means. Such an interpretive model has produced two negative results within African American churches.

First, it has opened the door to a number of theological errors. One such error is the notion that Christ's finished work on the cross was insufficient to

---

[41] As quoted in Cleophus J. LaRue, *The Heart of Black Preaching* (Louisville, KY: Westminster John Knox, 2000), 3, 18.

[42] James H. Cone, *A Black Theology of Liberation* (Maryknoll, NY: Orbis, 1990), 1.

[43] Farmer, *Beyond the Impasse*, 104.

[44] Ibid., 103.

[45] Ibid., 104.

provide eternal security. Due in part to the strong pull from "Word of Faith" ministries, some African American pulpits fail to give credible witness to the Bible's teaching on the eternal benefits of salvation. The Scriptures that speak of salvation being God's gift of eternal life[46] are ignored in favor of misrepresenting the original intent of Hebrews 6:4–6:

> For it is impossible for those who were once enlightened, and have tasted of the heavenly gift, and were made partakers of the Holy Ghost, and have tasted the good word of God, and the powers of the world to come, if they shall fall away, to renew them again unto repentance; seeing they crucify to themselves the Son of God afresh, and put him to an open shame.

These three verses are among the most difficult to comprehend in the entire Bible. All theological schools of thought have faced problems when trying to explain them consistently, and no Bible student is able to approach these verses with a completely neutral mind.[47] For those who preach "eternal security," it must be strange to find such strong warnings against apostasy. For those who believe Christians can lose their salvation, it must be just as challenging to read that such a falling away is permanent. It is quite evident that problems have arisen in connection with the various interpretations.

Given the context of spiritual maturity, there are really only two possible interpretations. On one hand, this passage could be teaching that those who profess Christ but do not actually possess Christ may become apostates. On the other hand, this passage could be encouraging those truly born again to go on to spiritual maturity since they cannot start their Christian lives over again. To do so would mean crucifying Christ afresh.

If biblical salvation is the central idea of the passage, then yes, given the wording, it seems to suggest that one can lose their salvation. However upon careful analysis the issue is not salvation after all. The main thrust is spiritual maturity as evidenced by the overall context.

Congregations need to be assured that the words being uttered from the pulpit are God's authoritative Word and not the preacher's own personal opinions. As James Berkley reminds preachers, "Our task is not to dazzle people with ideas that no one could ever imagine were hidden away behind the text.

---

[46] Two passages that speak precisely to the matter of God's gift of eternal life to repentant sinners are: John 3:16 ("For God so loved the world, that he gave his only begotten Son, that whosoever believeth in him, should not perish, but have everlasting life") and Romans 6:23 ("For the wages of sin is death; but the gift of God is eternal life through Jesus Christ our Lord").

[47] Homer A. Kent Jr., *The Epistle to the Hebrews* (Grand Rapids, MI: Baker, 1972), 107.

Rather, we must demonstrate how they too can read the Bible with understanding and apply it to their lives with integrity."[48]

Another negative result of reading personal biases and presuppositions into the biblical text is abuse of Scripture's teaching on spiritual gifts. Influenced by the preaching of Full Gospel ministers, many African American churches have succumbed to their system of belief.

The Full Gospel Baptist Church Fellowship International (FGBFI), the principal voice of Full Gospel preaching among African Americans, states,

> We believe in the perpetual and continuing ecclesiastical value of all spiritual gifts for the edification of the body of Christ until the end of this Church Age, which will be consummated by the return of our Lord Jesus Christ (Ephesians 4:11–13; 1 Corinthians 12–14, Romans 12).[49]

While all Christians agree that spiritual gifts are in operation in the church today, theologians are divided regarding the so-called "sign gifts" such as speaking in tongues, interpretation of tongues, healing, and some forms of prophecy. The theological position endorsed by Full Gospel supporters is the charismatic position. They contend that all gifts are operative today and are given just as they were in the early church. They believe that in order to experience the fullness of the Holy Spirit, all the spiritual gifts should be exercised in every local church. Many holding this position profess having had some kind of charismatic experience at one time or another.

Many conservative theologians justifiably object to the idea of continuation of the sign gifts, critiquing the continuationists' hermeneutics. As Larry Gilbert notes,

> Not all spiritual gifts are valid today, therefore speaking in tongues and interpretation of tongues should not be exercised in any church. It is also maintained that these gifts were given to the early church to establish or validate the authority of those who had the gift, and they

---

[48] James D. Berkley, ed., *Leadership Handbook of Preaching and Worship: Practical Insight from a Cross Section of Ministry Leaders* (Grand Rapids, MI: Baker, 1992), 19.

[49] *What We Believe: Full Gospel Distinctives*, Article II. The Full Gospel Baptist Fellowship International is a fellowship of churches and individuals that accepts the operation of all spiritual gifts (*the charismata*) in the church today. It was founded by Bishop Paul S. Morton Sr. in 1994. He currently serves as its presiding bishop. The fellowship's headquarters is in Atlanta, and its website is www.fullgospelbaptist.org. Traditional Full Gospel teaching can be traced back to 1906–1908 as a movement spawned from the Azusa Street revivals. William Seymour (1870–1922) is believed to be the father of both the Pentecostal and Full Gospel movements and their emphasis on the baptism with (of) the Holy Ghost, particularly with evidence of speaking in tongues. See, Anyabwile, *The Decline of African-American Theology*, 38–39, 195–201.

were phased out by the end of the first century with the completion
of the Canon of Scripture.[50]

Sound exegesis is important because it enables the preacher to stay within
the text's original historical, grammatical, and theological meaning. As we
have seen, such an approach would help African American churches avoid
several common pitfalls.

DISCUSSION QUESTIONS

1. What is the most important aspect of bridging the gap between the ancient
   biblical text and the contemporary audience?
2. Explain how Jesus Christ is the "exegesis" of God the Father.
3. Why is correct exegesis important to accurate biblical exposition?
4. What difficulties can arise if we subscribe to the "multiple meanings of the
   text" philosophy?
5. Some believe the meaning of a Bible text is determined exclusively by the
   reader. Do you agree? Explain.
6. Explain the dangers of reading personal biases into a biblical text.

---

[50] Larry Gilbert, *Team Ministry: A Guide to Spiritual Gifts and Lay Involvement* (Lynchburg,
VA: Church Growth Institute, 1987), 64.

3

A Theology of Preaching

*Careful, meditative, and painstaking exegesis must be the
foundation for an expository ministry. All doctrine and theology
with its attendant application must be the result of a literal,
grammatical, historical, contextual, redemptive comprehension of
the sacred text. Any attempt at preaching apart from this a priori
commitment is to undercut the very substance of proclamation.*[1]

OUR present culture presents unique challenges to preachers. The
need for sound biblical preaching is the same today as in Bible times.
People are still sinners and need a Word from the Lord. Today's
preachers, however, face an onslaught of distinctive challenges which can be
turned into opportunities for spiritual productivity. The preacher must rise to
the challenge and target both the mind and heart of his listening audience. As
Donald G. Miller rightly notes,

> To preach the gospel is not merely to say words but to effect a deed.
> To preach is not merely to stand in a pulpit and speak, no matter how
> eloquently and effectively, not even to set forth a theology, no matter
> how clearly it is stated nor how worthy the theology. To preach is to
> become part of a dynamic event wherein the living, redeeming God
> reproduces his act of redemption in a living encounter with men
> through the preacher. True preaching is an extension of the Incarna-
> tion into the contemporary moment, the transfiguring of the Cross
> and the resurrection from ancient facts of a remote past into living

---

[1] Arturo G. Azurdia III, *Spirit Empowered Preaching* (Great Britain: Christian Focus,
2003), 11.

realities of the present. A sermon is an act wherein the crucified, risen Lord personally confronts men either to save or to judge them. In a real sermon, then, Christ is the Preacher. The Preacher speaks through the preacher.[2]

Preaching must reflect accurately the biblical text and at the same time be culturally relevant. In this chapter a theology of preaching will be explored. We will see that God is the originator of preaching. He ordained it and expects it to be the primary means whereby his will is communicated to his people. Our discussion will cover the nature of biblical preaching, the ethos of preaching in the African American tradition, and the value of expository preaching. Each topic will be examined in light of biblical teaching.

THE NATURE OF BIBLICAL PREACHING

Biblical preaching has been defined in narrow terms as "the proclamation of the gospel"[3] and in broad terms as "the oral communication of Biblical truth by the Holy Spirit through a human personality to a given audience with the intent of enabling a positive response."[4] David Olford of the Stephen Olford Center for Biblical Preaching remarked that preaching is the "activity of communicating and proclaiming a message from God, a message derived from the content of the Scriptures."[5]

Biblical preaching has also been defined as "textual-thematic exposition" because the sermon's theme (subject) is to be rooted in the text.[6] The purpose of textual-thematic exposition is to communicate in a way that corresponds with what God has said and can be understood and responded to by those listening in an appropriate fashion.

The nature of biblical preaching is best understood when its importance in God's agenda for redeeming humanity is examined, including the mission and message of the preacher. A key text in this regard is 1 Corinthians 1:17–21:

> For Christ sent me not to baptize, but to preach the gospel: not with wisdom of words, lest the cross of Christ should be made of none effect. For the preaching of the cross is to them that perish foolishness; but unto us which are saved it is the power of God. For it

---

[2] Donald G. Miller, *Fire in Thy Mouth* (1954; repr., Grand Rapids, MI: Baker, 1976), 17.

[3] John MacArthur, Jr., *Rediscovering Pastoral Ministry* (Dallas, TX: Word, 1995), 250.

[4] Jerry Vines, *Power in the Pulpit* (Chicago, IL: Moody, 1999), 27.

[5] David Olford, *Essentials of Expository Preaching: The Purpose of Biblical Preaching* (Memphis, TN: Olford Ministries International, 2005), 19.

[6] Sidney Greidanus, *The Modern Preacher and the Ancient Text: Interpreting and Preaching Biblical Literature* (Grand Rapids, MI: Eerdmans, 1988), 122.

is written, I will destroy the wisdom of the wise, and will bring to nothing the understanding of the prudent. Where is the wise? where is the scribe? where is the disputer of this world? hath not God made foolish the wisdom of this world? For after that in the wisdom of God the world by wisdom knew not God, it pleased God by the foolishness of preaching to save them that believe.

Paul was writing to the saints at Corinth to explain the nature of his preaching ministry. The Corinthian church's sectarian spirit had created division among the church body, and Paul needed to admonish them regarding his mission and the divine origin and content of his message. Paul's admonition serves as a reminder to all preachers.

The Mission of the Preacher

As God's appointed mouthpiece, Paul's mission to the Corinthians was Christological. Paul said, "For Christ sent me not to baptize, but to preach the gospel" (v. 17a). This statement met head-on the disunity which had erupted within the Corinthian congregation. While the believers jostled over who their favorite preachers were, Paul reprimanded them for creating disunity. He appealed to them on the basis of Christological truth as he asked rhetorically, "Is Christ divided?" The obvious answer was "no," for there was but one Christ. For these believers to form factions within their midst was to deny the unity of Christ and his church.

In view of the sectarianism within the church, Paul was quick to state that his main mission was not to baptize but to proclaim the gospel of Jesus Christ. Paul did not minimize water baptism. Quite the contrary! He had previously mentioned a few names of persons he baptized (see 1 Cor 1:14, 16). Paul's point was to articulate the true nature of his mission. He was not appointed by Christ to baptize but to preach the gospel.

The word Paul used for "preach" in verse 17 is the Greek word *euanggelizo*, which means "to announce good news." As a preacher, Paul had been commissioned by Christ to be a proclaimer of good news, the good news of salvation through Jesus Christ. This was his primary mission, with every other aspect of ministry being secondary. While the church at Corinth probably had many ministry needs, Paul's primary mission to them had been to preach the gospel, "not with wisdom of words, lest the cross of Christ should be made of none effect" (v. 17b).

The Message of the Preacher

In verses 18–21, Paul explained the content of his message, namely, the cross of Jesus Christ. It's interesting that three different words for "preaching" occur in this chapter. In verse 17, as we have seen, the word is *euanggelizo*, meaning "to announce good news." In verse 18, preaching is referred to as the "word (*logos*) of the cross," which notes the divine nature of the message preached as well as its communication. The word used for "preach" in verse 23 is *kerusso*, which emphasizes the act of publicly proclaiming the message of God.[7] Paul is stating unequivocally that his message content was Christ's cross and not human wisdom.

Personal Observation

Every man called of God to preach has been commissioned to preach the gospel of Jesus Christ. Both his mission and message have Christ as their focus, with an aim to save sinners and edify saints. Preachers, including those in African American churches, must recognize the awesome responsibility that has been placed on them. God has called them to be good news bearers, watchmen, signalers, and trumpet blowers in light of potential dangers that lurk about. Two passages of Scripture demonstrate the urgency of the task.

The first passage, Romans 10:13–15, deals with the urgent need for preachers to preach the gospel:

> For whosoever shall call upon the name of the Lord shall be saved. How then shall they call on him in whom they have not believed? And how shall they believe in him of whom they have not heard? And how shall they hear without a preacher? And how shall they preach, except they be sent? As it is written, how beautiful are the feet of them that preach the gospel of peace, and bring glad tidings of good things!

The requirement of faithfulness in preaching is based on the reality that where there is no preaching, there will be no hearing; where there is no hearing, there will be no believing; and where there is no believing, there will be no souls saved.

The second passage, Ezekiel 33:1–7, deals with preaching that warns the people of God:

---

[7] Paige Patterson, *The Troubled Triumphant Church: An Exposition of First Corinthians* (Nashville, TN: Thomas Nelson, 1983), 31.

> Again the word of the LORD came unto me saying, Son of man,
> speak to the children of thy people, and say unto them, when I bring
> the sword upon a land, if the people of the land take a man of their
> coasts, and set him for their watchman: If when he seeth the sword
> come upon the land, he blow the trumpet, and warn the people; Then
> whosoever hearth the sound of the trumpet, and taketh not warning;
> if the sword come, and take him away, his blood shall be upon his
> own head. He heard the sound of the trumpet, and took not warning;
> his blood shall be upon him. But he that taketh warning shall deliver
> his soul. But if the watchman see the sword come, and blow not the
> trumpet, and the people be not warned; if the sword come, and take
> away any person from among them, he is taken away of his iniquity;
> but his blood will I require at the watchman's hand. So thou, O son
> of man, I have set thee a watchmen unto the house of Israel; there-
> fore thou shalt hear the word at my mouth, and warn them from me.

God told his prophet Ezekiel that if he sounded the alarm of impending danger and the people failed to take heed, their blood would be on their own hands. If, however, he failed to sound the alarm, then the people's blood would be on his hands. It would appear then that the fate of the people was dependent, in part, on Ezekiel's faithfulness in discharging his duties.

The black preacher must be convinced of his calling to admonish the people of God with the Word of God. He has not been called to entertain or mesmerize his listeners. God's people need the Bible to "reprove, rebuke and exhort" (2 Tim 4:2) and encourage them in their walk with Christ. God has designed his Word to be the primary source for his people's victory over sin, their spiritual growth, their theological stability, and their equipping for Christian service.

This is the challenge facing all preachers. In spite of the fact that there is a crisis in preaching, in spite of the fact some preachers are making a shipwreck of their calling, in spite of the growing numbers of people who disdain wholesome Bible preaching, it is incumbent upon the preacher to begin preaching from the conviction that he is the medium and his preaching is the means God chose to communicate his Word and will to humanity.

THE ETHOS OF PREACHING IN THE
AFRICAN AMERICAN CONTEXT

The African American preacher is an important figure in the lives of black people, and his preaching is the centerpiece of worship in the black church. The average person fails to recognize just how significant the church is for African Americans. For one, the African American church is the one institution where average black people are in full control. They control the preaching, sing-ing, leadership, and finances. Most every other aspect of society is dominated by whites or the rich and famous. In addition, the black church serves a social purpose, bringing together people who share the same struggles, persecutions, and fears. In the middle of this is the phenomenon known as black preaching.

Traditionally, and perhaps in the minds of most black preachers, black preaching is not so much taught as it is caught. It is developed over time as the preacher immerses himself in African American economic, political, social, and religious life.[8] Historically, African American preachers were mostly self-taught until college and seminary training became available.[9]

The Christian community must never forget that the religious life of Afri-can Americans was brewed in a cauldron of segregation and injustice. Black preaching was produced in that same cauldron. What emerged was a tradition of worship and preaching exclusive to African Americans. In his book *Black Preaching*, Henry Mitchell expounds on the uniqueness of black preaching:

> Black preaching and worship grew out of the oral culture and corpo-rate experiences shared by African worship practices and communal living. Heavy emphasis is often placed on the sonority and musical-ity of oral communication in communal patterns of participation. Racist conditions that limited or even prohibited reading the Bible and freely gathering in churches quite unintentionally, but directly, contributed to the underground insurgence of these black church traditions.[10]

In *The Negro Church*, sociologist E. Franklin Frazier shared his perspec-tive on black preaching by affirming,

> Perhaps one of the more direct historical factors in the use of the Bible in black preaching grew out of the constrictions imposed by slaveholders and white churches. Slaves became increasingly familiar with the Bible through black preachers who would inter-pret Scripture through the dramatization of the biblical story and its application to African-American life. This use and interpretation of the Bible eventually became the slaves' primary means of adapting Christianity.[11]

---

[8] Willette Burgie-Bryant, *More Power in the Pulpit: How America's Most Effective Black Preachers Prepare Their Sermons* (Louisville, KY: Westminster John Knox, 2009), 1–2.

[9] Henry H. Mitchell, *Black Preaching: The Recovery of a Powerful Art* (Nashville, TN: Abingdon, 1990), 87.

[10] Ibid., 30–31.

[11] E. Franklin Frazier, *The Negro Church in America* (New York, NY: Schocken, 1963), 10–11. Edward Franklin Frazier (1894–1962) was an African-American sociologist, historian,

Worship style in an African American context can be summed up in one word: *freedom*. Worship in the predominately black church is not bound by any set of religious traditions or church bylaws. Rather, it is grounded on the premise that the Bible does not endorse any particular worship style. As long as worship is not pretentious (Luke 18:9–14), is according to spirit and truth (John 4:24), and centers on Christ's mission and message (Col 1:18–29), each church is entitled to develop its own unique style, according to the black church tradition. Preaching in the black church context occurs where there is freedom to worship in a style created for a church's unique personality.

Preaching in the African American context is extremely important in the lives of many black people. At least two factors have contributed to the phenomenon known as black preaching: preaching styles and participatory proclamation.

Preaching Styles

Preaching styles in the black church vary to some extent depending on the preacher's background, training, and denominational affiliation. Some black preachers use the lecture style while others are more demonstrative in their presentation. Regardless of the style, one thing is certain: preaching in the African American context is unique. Two realities have contributed to this uniqueness. First, it grabs the attention and incites the emotions of listeners. Second, it occurs in a context of celebration similar to what the Israelites experienced in the Old Testament. The celebratory nature of black preaching means the preaching event usually ends in a celebratory tone.[12]

While preaching styles vary somewhat, there is one prominent style in black churches that bears mentioning. That style is called the "whooping"[13] style. It occurs when the preacher's words begin taking on a musical quality. There is an obvious connection between singing and whooping. As the sermon unfolds, it begins to take a melodic and rhythmic shape.

---

and college professor. He taught at Morehouse College (Atlanta, GA), Fisk University (Nashville, TN), and Howard University (Washington, DC).

[12] For additional insight into the celebratory nature of black preaching, see: Henry H. Mitchell, *Celebration and Experience in Preaching*, rev. ed. (Nashville, TN: Abingdon, 2008), and, James Henry Harris, *The Word Made Plain: The Power and Promise of Preaching* (Minneapolis, MN: Augsburg Fortress, 2004).

[13] Of "Whooping," see: Martha Simmons and Frank Thomas, eds., *Preaching with Sacred Fire: An Anthology of African-American Sermon 1750 to the Present* (New York, NY: Norton, 2010) and John M. Spencer, *Sacred Symphony: The Chanted Sermons of the Black Preacher* (Westport, CT: Praeger, 1987).

The whooping style can be compared to a jetliner about to take off. The jetliner approaches the runway with normal speed, then pauses momentarily before it starts its journey down the runway. As it proceeds, it accelerates, going faster and faster until it lifts off. The whooping style is similar. It begins with a normal voice tone and pitch. As the sermon progresses, it starts to gain momentum. The preacher's voice begins to accelerate with rhythmic cadence. At the right moment, the voice and cadence lifts off. Both preacher and listeners soar into heights of exuberant, celebratory praise.

The whoop represents much of the preaching disseminated from African American pulpits. Many believe the whooping style of preaching is part of African American heritage.

Participatory Proclamation

The second factor responsible for the phenomenon known as black preaching is participatory proclamation. Most African American preachers will acknowledge that preaching is conversation. The preacher carries on a conversation with his audience. He engages them with words of admonition, expecting some form of response in return.

The anticipated response is verbal and usually takes shape in phrases such as, "Amen, my brother," "Say that, preacher," or "Tell the truth, preacher man." These phrases are spoken publicly, and are always directed toward the preacher. Such verbal response affects the preacher. It motivates and inspires him to keep preaching. Louis Lomax, in *The Negro Revolt*, commented briefly on participatory proclamation during his discussion of a 1955 Martin Luther King sermon in Montgomery, Alabama. As King began to preach, the people responded back to him this way:

King (K):   "There comes a time when people get tired."
Audience (A):   "Yes, Lord."
(K)   "We are here this evening to say to those who have mistreated us for so long that we are tired."
(A):   "Help him, Jesus!"
(K):   "We are tired of being segregated and humiliated."
(A):   "Amen."
(K):   " .... tired! ... did you hear me when I said 'tired'?"
(A):   "Yes, Lord!"[14]

---

[14] Louis E. Lomax, *The Negro Revolt* (New York, NY: Harper and Row, 1962), 90–91.

The give and take nature of communication between preacher and listener usually continues until the preaching event has concluded. Such participatory proclamation can be found in most African American churches.

Newcomers to African American worship typically notice an excitement not experienced in predominately white worship services. This is not to suggest African American worship is inherently better than other cultural expressions of worship. It is just different. Most settings where black preaching occurs are highly emotional. The hymns sung and prayers offered provide an adequate foundation for participatory proclamation. Days, weeks, months, and years of oppression experienced by both preacher and parishioner interface during the preaching event. Emotions run high and the excitement is overwhelming. As the preacher rises to proclaim God's Word, the waiting congregation is eager and ready to participate in the preaching event.

Cleophus LaRue argues, "Effective preaching can only happen when pulpit and pew are united in conversation with one another."[15] Pastor Frank Thomas refers to participatory proclamation as "dialogical language."[16] The preacher engages the people in the sermon, inviting them to be part of it and invest in it. When listeners invest in the sermon, they experience "the gospel more deeply and profoundly."[17] As Thomas notes,

> In the classical rationalistic deduction method, it was as if the minis-
> ter had come down from Mt. Sinai with a message from God, while
> the people waited passively for the revelation. But when dialogical
> language is used effectively, the people and the minister go up to
> the mountain of God together and encounter the word of God. If we
> are concerned about emotional process, we must use language that
> includes people.[18]

While the pastor engages in dialogical language, it is not uncommon for listeners to join him in the celebration by clapping or shouting. Such celebrative response to preaching reflects the soul's responsiveness to God for his bountiful blessings. It is in gratefulness to God that African American preachers and their congregants shout and celebrate during the preaching event. Ralph Wiley, in *Why Black People Tend to Shout*, says,

---

[15] Cleophus J. LaRue, ed., *More Power in the Pulpit: How America's Most Effective Black Preachers Prepare Their Sermons* (Louisville, KY: Westminster John Knox, 2009), 4.
[16] Frank A. Thomas, *They Like to Never Quit Praisin' God: The Role of Celebration in Preaching* (Cleveland, OH: The Pilgrim Press, 1997), 7.
[17] Ibid., 8.
[18] Ibid.

Black people tend to shout in churches, movie theaters, and any-where else they feel the need to shout, because when joy, pain, anger, confusion and frustration, ego and thought, mix it up, the way they do inside black people, the uproar is too big to hold inside. The feeling must be aired.[19]

The Negative Side of "Whooping"

While whooping preaching is extremely popular among African Amer-icans, there is at least one drawback associated with it. The whooping style gets people emotionally high but oftentimes lacks much biblical content. Some whooping preachers start out teaching the Bible but end up screaming about extra-biblical matters, expecting their listeners to respond emotionally. The results are predictable. People leave the worship service on an emotional high without having their minds and hearts spiritually challenged or awakened. Some listeners have no clue what the preacher's message was about. All they know is that the message made them feel good about themselves.

Worship can become distorted when the antics of the preacher replace Jesus Christ, the One who deserves center stage. Worship can become polluted when the truth of God is relegated to a subservient position in favor of the "whoop." If, while whooping, the preacher fails to disclose biblical truth, he has polluted or watered down the Bible's message.

Preachers should never whoop for the sake of whooping, and listeners should never shout because it's fashionable or because "everyone else does it." Every aspect of worship in the African American context should be biblically based, God-honoring, Christ-centered, and Holy Spirit-driven.

On a more positive note, the African American church has been blessed with preachers who, by God's matchless grace, were able to blend sound bibli-cal exposition and the whooping style. To them it was never a matter of either/ or, but of both/and. The list of such preachers includes E. V. Hill, G. E. Patter-son, E. K. Bailey, Manuel Scott, Jasper Williams, and Howard John Wesley. Their tremendous oratory skills, ability to correctly handle the biblical text, and colorful use of the English language gave listeners the impression these preachers had a direct pipeline to the mind of God. None of them sacrificed biblical truth on the altar of their preaching style.

It is noteworthy that when people think of African American preaching, they normally think solely of a particular preaching style. They think about an emotionally filled, "hyped up" enthusiastic worship experience. Yet great

---

[19] Ralph Wiley, *Why Black People Tend to Shout* (New York, NY: Penguin, 1991), 1.

preaching is never marked exclusively by its style. It announces the Word of God to those who live life on the edge with their backs up against the wall.

Preaching in the African American context verifies that the preached Word is something beyond the words of the preacher. African Americans long to hear the Word of God in terms that relate to their current situation. They believe that when the preacher preaches, he delivers a transforming, liberating Word from God—a Word that addresses their current stressful circumstances and gives them hope for the future.

THE VALUE OF EXPOSITORY PREACHING

"There is no such entity as 'the best sermon form.' Sermons can take various forms, but no preaching form came down from heaven."[20] How does one commend expository preaching without intimating that other preaching methods lack merit? Perhaps the best way to begin is by stating unequivocally that every preaching method has some merit. Yet, while each preaching method has its own uniqueness and value, it is this writer's opinion that the expository method represents the most effective way of fulfilling Paul's command to "preach the word" (2 Tim 4:2).

Bible Exposition

The preaching event is the "activity of communicating and proclaiming a message from God, a message derived from the content of the Scriptures."[21] Preaching's objective is not to highlight the presuppositions and opinions of the preacher. The specific purpose of the preaching event is to communicate a specific message derived from a specific text or specific texts of Scripture, and to "call forth the response appropriate to that message."[22]

Biblical preaching is the proclamation or heralding of God's Word, explaining it, opening it up to others, making it clear so the people of God can hear it and apply it to their individual lives. Preaching entails expounding God's truth to the hearts and lives of God's people. Preaching is the exposition of the Word of God.

Exposition conveys the idea of exposing something. According to Webster, "exposition" is a "discourse designed to convey information or explain

---

[20] Haddon W. Robinson and Torrey W. Robinson, *It's All in How You Tell It: Preaching First-Person Expository Messages* (Grand Rapids, MI: Baker, 2003), 10.

[21] Olford, *Essentials of Expository Preaching*, 19.

[22] Ibid.

what is difficult to understand."[23] Applied to preaching, an exposition is the laying open of the biblical text to public view in order to set forth its meaning. Exposition is, as John MacArthur says, "explaining what is difficult to understand and making appropriate application."[24]

Expository preaching provides an opportunity to fully explain the biblical text from start to finish. It creates an atmosphere where the preacher is compelled to study the text's historical, grammatical, and theological significance. The outcome is phenomenal. The preacher's ministry is enhanced as his sermons are textually based and not unduly influenced by personal, political, or cultural agendas.

What is expository preaching and why is it so effective? Two sources answer these questions well.

Ramesh Richard and Expository Preaching

The first source is the definition of expository preaching offered by Ramesh Richard. He defines it as "the contemporization of the central proposition of a biblical text that is derived from proper methods of interpretation, and declared through effective means of communication to inform minds, instructs hearts, and influence behavior toward godliness."[25]

Richard's definition highlights the importance of moving from exegesis to exposition via a three-step process that includes contemporization, interpretation, and communication. By contemporization is meant the taking of what was written centuries ago and making it meaningful to present-day audiences. This is not some form of "upgrading the Bible because the Bible is already relevant to human issues."[26] By interpretation is meant the study of the biblical text to understand its meaning. The communication aspect is the verbal connection between the preacher and the contemporary audience. All three aspects are vital to expository preaching in the contemporary culture.

Historically, in many African American pulpits, expository preaching has not been the preferred method of sermon delivery. An allegorical method of preaching is preferred. This fits well in those pulpits where racial, economic, or political issues are dominant. Peter Paris, for example, believes Bible interpretation should take into consideration the years of struggle in the black

---

[23] *Webster's Ninth New Collegiate Dictionary* (Springfield, MA: Merriam Webster, 1988), 438.

[24] MacArthur, *Rediscovering Expository Preaching*, 11.

[25] Ramesh Richard, *Preparing Expository Sermons* (Grand Rapids, MI: Baker, 2001), 19.

[26] Ibid.

experience.[27] From this mind-set, a new hermeneutical approach to Bible study and exposition has been formulated. Cleophus LaRue calls this approach the "hermeneutic of power"[28] and believes it serves as the template for the creation and organization of the typical black sermon.[29]

Without regard for many of the principles associated with sound exegetical study, this new hermeneutical approach yields sermons which address the external needs of people while leaving their souls floundering in spiritual darkness and ignorance. It is the duty of preachers to proclaim God's truth so it can, as says, "inform minds, instructs hearts, and influence behavior toward godliness."

Stephen Olford and Expository Preaching

The second source we must consider is the definition of expository preaching offered by the late Stephen Olford.[30] His grasp of biblical truth coupled with his flawless use of the English language made him an example of effective expositional preaching. Olford defined expository preaching as the Spirit-empowered explanation and proclamation of the text of God's Word, with due regard to the historical, contextual, grammatical and doctrinal significance of the given passage, with the specific object of invoking a Christ-transforming response.[31]

On the surface this definition seems quite wordy. Yet it helpfully reveals four aspects of an expository sermon: dependence on God, textual awareness, doctrinal focus, and practical purpose.

Dependence on God. For a sermon to be expositional, the preacher must be totally dependent on God, a reality Olford references as "the Spirit-empowered explanation and proclamation of the text of God's Word."[32] The Holy Spirit plays the key role in both sermon preparation and proclamation. In sermon preparation the Holy Spirit is the illuminator. He illuminates the truth from God's Word to the mind and heart of the preacher. He is, as the Bible says, the One who "searcheth all things, yea, the deep things of God" (1 Cor 2:10). Who better to know and understand the mind and Word of God than God himself?

---

[27] Paris, *The Social Teaching of the Black Churches*, 10.
[28] LaRue, *The Heart of Black Preaching*, 68.
[29] Ibid.
[30] In 2004 I attended the Stephen Olford School of Biblical Preaching in Memphis, Tennessee, and in 2005 graduated as a Fellow of the Institute of Biblical Preaching.
[31] Olford, *Essentials of Expository Preaching*, 33.
[32] Ibid.

The Holy Spirit also prepares the hearts of both the preacher and listener to receive God's truth. As they submit to the Holy Spirit, yielding their lives to his control, the preacher and listener are able to "receive with meekness the engrafted word, which is able to save [their] souls" (Jas 1:21). The word "engrafted" is the Greek word *emphyton* and refers to that which has been planted. God's Word is to be ingrown or inborn, rooted in the fertile soil of a soul in right relationship with the Holy Spirit.[33] As the preacher exhibits a life of godliness, he becomes the mouthpiece of God.

In sermon proclamation the Holy Spirit is the active agent. He not only fills the heart, mind, and mouth of the preacher, He also assists listeners in grasping the truth of God's Word. When referring to his preaching ministry in Thessalonica, Paul reminded his readers of the demonstration of the Holy Spirit's power through his preaching: "For our gospel came not unto you in word only, but also in power, and in the Holy Ghost, and in much assurance; as you know what manner of men we were among you for your sake" (1 Thess 1:5). Paul's message to the saints at Thessalonica came in the power of the Holy Spirit. His message was marked not by cleverness or human biases but by the demonstration of the power of God. The Holy Spirit brought God's Word home to the hearts of His people.

For a sermon to be labeled expository, the preacher must fully rely on the ministry of the Holy Spirit in both his sermon preparation and proclamation. This creates within the preacher a passion for preaching God's Word. Pastor Alex Montoya argues that the secret to passionate preaching is spiritual power.[34] He elaborates on his conviction by saying to all communicators of God's Word,

> Ours is a spiritual work! We are not CEO's of some secular organization like Wal-Mart or IBM. We are God's ministers called and authorized to proclaim His holy Word, a Word that God describes as "living and active and sharper than any two-edged sword, and piercing as far as the division of soul and spirit, of both joints and marrow, and able to judge the thoughts and intentions of the heart" (Heb. 4:12). Spiritual work demands spiritual power.[35]

Montoya's comments reflect the sentiments of countless preachers who know the benefit of passionate preaching and living in the power of the Spirit.

---

[33] John F. Walvoord and Roy B. Zuck, *The Bible Knowledge Commentary: New Testament* (Colorado Springs, CO: David C. Cook, 1983), 823.

[34] Alex Montoya, *Preaching with Passion* (Grand Rapids, MI: Kregel, 2000), 21.

[35] Ibid.

Living in the Spirit enables the preacher to be passionate about God. When he is passionate about God, he will be passionate in his preaching.[36]

Textual Awareness. The second aspect of expository preaching is textual awareness. Olford refers to this in his definition by saying an expository sermon is the "proclamation of the text of God's Word, with due regard to the historical, contextual, grammatical and doctrinal significance of the given passage."

Two words that stand out in this portion of the definition are "text" and "contextual." Both make reference to God's Word, the Bible, and both reflect this essential aspect of preparing and delivering expository sermons. By "text" is meant the verses, paragraph, or literary unit selected to be studied and preached. Context refers to the meaning of the verses, paragraphs, and books surrounding the passage being studied. Preaching, as Haddon Robinson notes, should focus on "the big idea," of the text being preached, the central truth that the text proclaims.[37]

In his book *Anointed Expository Preaching*, Olford notes the importance of textual awareness: "At the heart of expository preaching is a commitment to expose and explain the truth that is there in the text of God's Word. A primary and fundamental concern in sermon preparation is to discern accurately the truth that is really in the text."[38]

Textual awareness requires diligent and thorough study of what the text says in light of its background, history, language, and context. The preacher's exegetical approach will seek to uncover what the text says and not what he wants it to say. This will safeguard against forcing his own biases and presuppositions into the text. As a consequence, the sermon is rooted in the text itself. As Olford explains,

> The Scripture itself is not only stated to be the authority for the truth, it is shown, or exposed, as the authority for the truth. The truth of God is proclaimed and explained on the basis of textual explanation. The preacher is concerned that the message accurately corresponds with what God has said in His Word.[39]

Textual awareness should be a matter of concern for every communicator of God's Word. Yet the inclination to drift away from a text's intended meaning

[36] Ibid., 22.
[37] Haddon W. Robinson, *Biblical Preaching: The Development and Delivery of Expository Messages* (Grand Rapids, MI: Baker, 1980), 31–44.
[38] Stephen F. Olford, *Anointed Expository Preaching* (Nashville, TN: Broadman & Holman, 1998), 101–2.
[39] Ibid., 103.

is widespread among African American preachers. For example, some preachers address issues that directly affect their churches and communities without any regard for the meaning of the text supposedly under consideration. Such preaching distorts the text, sacrificing its intended truth on the altar of the preacher's biases.

Doctrinal Focus. The third aspect of expository preaching is its doctrinal focus. As Olford notes, expository preaching considers the "doctrinal significance" of the text. Doctrinal significance refers to a text's theological basis, the timeless truths it teaches about the triune Godhead and God's purpose and will for humanity. A focus on doctrinal significance guarantees that the sermon will be God-centered and not rooted in personal biases or presuppositions. As the preacher engages in exegesis, he discovers the mind and heart of God in the text. Most expositors agree with Pastor John Piper when he says,

> God himself is the necessary subject matter of our preaching, in his majesty and truth and holiness and righteousness and wisdom and faithfulness and sovereignty and grace. And by that I don't mean we shouldn't preach about nitty-gritty practical things like parenthood and divorce and AIDS and gluttony and television and sex. What I mean is that every one of those things should be swept right up into the holy presence of God and laid bare to the roots of its God-wardness or godlessness. It is not the job of the preacher to give people moral or psychological pep talks about how to get along in the world.[40]

Practical Purpose. The final aspect of expository preaching is its practical purpose. Expository preaching should have, as Olford suggests, "the specific object of invoking a Christ-transforming response." To "invoke" means to inspire, to motivate, or to arouse. Expository preaching must aim to transform people's lives. This is the practical side of preaching: the desire for people to have a personal encounter with God. Such an encounter should engender change in the life of a listener.

While encouraging the Thessalonian church regarding the powerful effects of God's Word, Paul said to them, "For this cause also thank we God without ceasing, because when ye received the word of God which ye heard of us, ye received it not as the word of men, but as it is in truth, the word of God, which effectually worketh also in you that believe" (1 Thess 2:13). As the saints at Thessalonica heard and believed God's Word, changes began to take place in their lives. Two words in this verse certify this truth. The first word is

[40] John Piper, *The Supremacy of God in Preaching* (Grand Rapids, MI: Baker, 2004), 15.

"receive," which is the Greek word *paralambano*, meaning, "to receive near to oneself." The second word is "effectually," which is derived from the Greek word *energeo* meaning, "to be active, at work, and efficient."[41]

As Paul preached the Word of God, the Thessalonians heard it and welcomed it into their hearts as truth from God. The results were astounding. Once received, God's Word became an active power that operated in the people's lives, changing their character and behavior. The Thessalonian Christians had a transforming response to the preached Word.

The expository sermon should result in the transformation of lives. As people hear the Bible, their minds are confronted with God's truth, their hearts are burdened by their own sinfulness, and their wills are prompted to welcome God's truth to effect a change in their lives.

EVIDENCE OF EXPOSITORY PREACHING

Does the Bible affirm an expository method of preaching? This writer believes it does and will attempt to defend that conviction from two passages of Scripture—one from the Old Testament and the other from the New Testament.

Old Testament Evidence

While the prophetic preaching ministry constitutes at least half of Old Testament teaching, one verse in particular highlights the expository preaching method. The verse is Nehemiah 8:8: "So they read in the book of the law of God distinctly, and gave the sense, and caused the people to understand the reading."

The immediate context of this verse is important to understanding its overall significance. The first seven chapters of Nehemiah primarily discuss the material needs of God's people, Israel. Nehemiah is the dominant character in these chapters and his main concerns are to rebuild the Jerusalem walls and repopulate the city. Now, beginning with chapter 8, the emphasis shifts from the material needs of the people to their spiritual needs. Ezra becomes the dominant person in the book.

It is important to note that Ezra had returned to Jerusalem several years before Nehemiah. His primary mission as a scribe was to teach the returning exiles the law of God. When he first arrived in Jerusalem, the spiritual condition of the people's lives was appalling (see Ezra 9:1–4; 10:2, 10). As he

---

[41] Robert L. Thomas, *Ephesians through Philemon*, vol. 11 of *The Expositor's Bible Commentary*, Frank E. Gaebelein, general editor (Grand Rapids, MI: Zondervan 1981), 257.

faithfully and prayerfully taught the people God's truth, they began to respond in obedience. Upon Nehemiah's arrival, the people were challenged to trust God and assist with the rebuilding of the Jerusalem walls.

An important principle throughout the books of Nehemiah and Ezra is that rebuilding the walls and temple and repopulating the city of Jerusalem would not bring glory to God if God's people were not spiritually healthy. The process of spiritual renewal among the Jews required the continual reintroduction of God's Word back into their society. The people were so excited about God's Word that they asked Ezra to continue to teach them. The text says, "And all the people gathered themselves together as one man into the street that was before the water gate; and they spake unto Ezra the scribe to bring the book of the law of Moses, which the LORD had commanded to Israel" (Neh 8:1).

One can only imagine the excitement and emotional fervor generated among the people as Ezra stood on a platform and began reading the law of Moses. In response, the people stood up and began to praise God. The text says,

> And Ezra opened the book in the sight of all people; (for he was above all the people) and when he opened it, all the people stood up: And Ezra blessed the LORD, the great God. And all the people answered, Amen, Amen, with lifting up their hands: and they bowed their heads, and worshipped the LORD with their faces to the ground. (Neh 8:5–6)

But much more than reading the law was required. To encourage obedience among God's people, his Word also needed to be explained and applied. These are the three components of Old Testament expository preaching.

Reading the Bible with Clarity. The text says, "So they read in the book of the law of God distinctly" (v. 8a). The word "distinctly" is derived from the Hebrew word *parash*, meaning "to disperse, to specify, and to separate." The general idea is that of dispersing something in a clear manner.[42] Ezra the priest saw to it that God's Word was read (dispersed) clearly.

Expository preaching begins with the public reading of God's Word in a clear manner. This is by far the most important aspect of any worship service. The public reading of God's Word sets the tone and creates an atmosphere for true worship. As the preacher reads God's Word, listeners are brought face-to-face with the text's movement and flow of thought. If he reads his text passionately and meaningfully, listeners will grow to appreciate it and recognize

---

[42] Merrill F. Unger, *Unger's Commentary on the Old Testament* (Chattanooga, TN: AMG International, 2002), 647.

that God's Word is not antiquated or out of date. Rather, they will see it as an exciting, relevant Word. It is incumbent upon preachers to read their preaching text with clarity.

Explaining the Bible with Precision. The text goes on to say they "gave the sense." Ezra made certain God's Word made sense to the people. The word "sense" is the word *sekel* and refers to giving understanding. In giving the sense, Ezra provided the people an understanding of what the law of God meant.

Expository preaching involves explaining the meaning of the text. The text means something by what it says, and the preacher is responsible for bringing its intended meaning to the forefront of his message. John Stott calls this type of exposition a form of "bridge-building."[43] That is, it seeks to bring together the original meaning of the text and the contemporary audience.

Before people can apply God's Word to their lives, they must know what it means. Far too much preaching begins and ends with application with no regard for the text's intended meaning. It's one thing for Christians to know what the Bible says and quite another for them to know what it means. Giving the sense is required and should be expected in Bible exposition.

Applying the Bible with Accuracy. Nehemiah 8:8 further states that they "caused the people to understand the reading." "Understand" translates the Hebrew word *bene*, meaning "to distinguish, to discern, or to deal wisely."[44] As Ezra read and explained the law of God, he also provided adequate application of it. To cause the people to understand God's law meant more than merely providing them information about what it said. It meant taking what was read and explained and relating its significance to the everyday life of the Israelites.

Expository preaching requires life application. This is the "so what?" of the sermon. This enables the audience to ask and answer questions like, "What did the preacher preach about?" "What difference does it make?" and "What do I need to do with what was preached?"

The truths preached must be related to the everyday life situations of the listeners. The expository preaching event creates an interaction between God's truth and people's lives. Truth and life connect at the right moment, establishing an environment conducive to life change. Expository preaching should become a life-changing event, as evidenced by the Old Testament.

---

[43] John Stott, *Between Two Worlds* (Grand Rapids, MI: Eerdmans, 1982), 135.
[44] W. E. Vine, *Vine's Complete Expository Dictionary of Old and New Testament Words* (Nashville, TN: Thomas Nelson, 1996), 273.

New Testament Evidence

New Testament affirmation of expository preaching includes Acts 8, verses 29–31 in particular.

> Then the Spirit said unto Philip, Go near, and join thyself to this chariot. And Philip ran thither to him, and heard him read the prophet Isaiah, and said, Understandeth thou what thou readest? And he said, How can I, except some man should guide me? And he desired Philip that he would come up and sit with him.

The two characters in this narrative are Deacon Philip and the Ethiopian eunuch. Deacon Philip had been compelled by the angel of the Lord to leave a thriving evangelistic campaign in Samaria and journey south to the Gaza desert. As he journeyed, he came upon an Ethiopian eunuch sitting in his chariot reading a portion of the Old Testament. Suddenly, God's Spirit commanded Philip to join the Ethiopian while he was reading.

As he approached the chariot, Philip heard him reading aloud from the book of Isaiah. Philip wanted the man to understand the truths he was reading, so he asked him, "Understandeth thou what thou readest?" The Ethiopian's response reveals what expositional preaching is designed to accomplish. He responded to Philip's question with a question: "How can I, except some man should guide me?"

The word "guide" is a translation of the Greek word *hodegeo*, which means "to lead the way."[45] The Ethiopian desperately needed someone to lead the way and unlock the truths of Scriptures so he could comprehend them. The truths under consideration were Isaiah's prophetic forecast of the coming Messiah and his ministry of suffering and death (see Isa 53:3–8).

God, in his sovereign design, has chosen some persons to open up the truths of Scripture for others. Harold Bryson says these "openers-of-the-Bible may be called expositors, for they expose the truth of God's Word."[46]

SUMMATION OF A THEOLOGY OF PREACHING

This chapter was devoted to a theology of preaching. Three subjects were discussed in light of biblical teaching.

This chapter began by discussing of the nature of biblical preaching. Preaching was defined as the oral communication of biblical truth. To understand its

---

[45] Vine, *Complete Expository Dictionary of Old and New Testament Words*, 285.
[46] Harold T. Bryson, *Expository Preaching: The Art of Preaching Through a Book of the Bible* (Nashville, TN: Broadman & Holman, 1995), 5.

nature, biblical preaching was explored in light of its importance in God's agenda for redeeming lost humanity. It was demonstrated that the mission of the preacher is to be Christ centered and not influenced by worldly wisdom.

The second subject discussed was the ethos of preaching in the African American context. Preaching styles and participatory proclamation were considered as two key aspects of traditional black preaching. While preaching style has some importance, it was established that great preaching is never defined by its stylistic components. It is about powerfully proclaiming the Bible.

The third subject discussed was the value of expository preaching. The definitions of expository preaching recommended by Ramesh Richard and Stephen F. Olford were scrutinized. It was concluded that expository sermons include four aspects: dependence on God, textual awareness, doctrinal focus, and practical purpose.

Biblical preaching is God's method of revealing to lost humanity the truth regarding his Son, Jesus Christ. The need for sound biblical preaching is the same today as in Bible times.

DISCUSSION QUESTIONS

1. What is a good definition of "preaching"?
2. Why is sound Bible preaching needed today, as it was in Bible times?
3. In 1 Corinthians, how does the apostle Paul describe the mission and message of the preacher?
4. How is today's preacher similar to the prophet Ezekiel, God's watchman on the wall?
5. What makes preaching in the African American church the centerpiece of worship?
6. Do you agree that "preaching style" is important to effectively communicating God's Word? Explain.
7. What is expository preaching and how does it differ from other preaching methods?
8. Note one example of expository preaching from the Old Testament and one from the New Testament.

4

Relevance in Biblical Preaching

*Today postmodernism says: All you can believe is what's
in your own heart, count on intuition and faith, give up
on the idea of truth, have an experience instead.*[1]

T HE importance of the preaching event should never be minimized
or taken for granted. As God's Word is communicated, hearts and
lives are challenged and changed for the glory of God. It is during
the preaching event that people are confronted with a word from heaven, a
word R. Albert Mohler describes as "awkward, challenging, and difficult."[2] It
is during the preaching event that the Bible's two sharp edges pierce the listener's mind, heart, and soul, thus effecting change.

The Bible is God's relevant Word. It is the powerful voice of God that, as
Paul put it, "effectually worketh also in you that believe" (1 Thess 2:13). God's
Word works! It accomplishes what God intends for it to accomplish. It therefore never needs to be made relevant. The Bible is God's relevant Word that
speaks to man regardless of where he is geographically, socially, culturally,
intellectually, or spiritually.

This chapter is devoted to studying the relevance of biblical preaching.
Three topics will be discussed. First, postmodernism and its effect on biblical

---

[1] Graham Johnston, *Preaching to a Postmodern World: A Guide to Reaching Twenty-First Century Listeners* (Grand Rapids, MI: Baker, 2001), 9.
[2] R. Albert Mohler Jr., *He Is Not Silent: Preaching in a Postmodern World* (Chicago, IL: Moody, 2008), 21.

preaching will be analyzed. Second, the concept known as "contextualization" will be defined and described. Third, comments from a cross section of preachers will be cited in discussing effective communication of God's Word.

POSTMODERNISM AND ITS EFFECT ON BIBLICAL PREACHING

Postmodernism is a worldview that argues absolute truth does not exist. In the mind of the average postmodernist, all belief systems are valid and no one system is more valid than others. Each person or group is therefore entitled to develop their own philosophy or worldview.

Basic Philosophy of Postmodernism

The root of postmodernism is the idea that absolute truth does not exist. A true postmodernist, then, denies that the Bible is God's authoritative Word. Truth to the postmodernist is relative. What is right or wrong for one person is not necessarily right or wrong for everyone. In its extreme form, postmodernism contends that the things society labels unlawful are not necessarily wicked. It's easy to understand why our nation so quickly alters its laws to accommodate drug use and same-sex marriages. Our government has been influenced by postmodernism. In fact, every segment of society has been negatively influenced by this disease. Not even the Christian church has been spared. Indeed, preachers have succumbed to postmodernism, and some have sacrificed preaching biblical truth on the altar of being relevant, practical, or preaching need-based messages. Theologian R. Albert Mohler Jr. comments on the danger of postmodernism and needs-based preaching:

> Urged on by devotees of "needs-based preaching," many evangelicals have abandoned the text without recognizing that they have done so. These preachers may eventually get to the text in the course of the sermon, but the text does not set the agenda or establish the shape of the message. The sacred desk has become an advice center, and the pew has become the therapist's couch. Psychological and practical concerns have displaced theological exegesis, and the preacher directs his sermon to the congregation's perceived needs rather to their need for a Savior.[3]

Tolerance, individualism, and moral relativism have all bloomed from the root of postmodernism. Tolerance is the idea that all views and opinions are of

---

[3] Mohler, *He Is Not Silent*, 20.

equal importance and should be considered as valid. Individualism insists that the individual is what really matters. A person's ideologies, opinions, goals, and interests take precedence over everything that threatens their ultimate expression. Moral relativism says no universal code of moral conduct exists. As a consequence, people should tolerate the beliefs and practices of others even if those beliefs and practices are in opposition to societal norms. Moral relativists argue that what is right or wrong can only be determined in context with one's personal value system.

A View from the Pew: The Mind of a Postmodernist

It is time for Christian churches to get back to the basics of preaching God's infallible Word. Postmodernity has caused many to question the Bible's authority as people struggle to determine what is right and what is wrong.

Hath God Said?

The postmodern mind-set has created a church culture of ignorance and doubt. The average church member leaves the church service asking, "Has God really spoken?" These words remind us of Satan's question to Eve in Genesis 3 when he challenged God's authority: "Yea, hath God said, ye shall not eat of every tree of the garden?" (Gen 3:1b). Such a question calls to mind Paul's warning to Timothy when he said, "For the time will come when they will not endure sound doctrine; but after their own lusts shall they heap to themselves teachers, having itching ears" (2 Tim 4:3). Timothy was warned of the coming apostasy that would sweep across Christendom, leaving in its path listeners who deliberately questioned the authority of God's Word.

Postmodernists believe God's voice is one of many credible voices deserving humanity's attention and consideration. They suggest the Bible is as good a book as the Quran or other religious writings. They would probably go so far as to suggest the Bible makes good reading material. Yet in the process of commending the Bible as a best-seller, the postmodernist would deny its authority.

According to postmodern philosophy, since truth is relative, each individual can craft his or her own brand of truth—one that serves personal interests. The end result is devastating. Morality becomes obsolete as people are encouraged to live by their own rules. Since every person's ethics and morals are legitimate, right and wrong are not absolute values. They are personalized according to one's circumstances or cultural orientation.

The average person's mind is inundated with postmodern ideology. It appears subliminally via the internet, television programming, and magazine articles, not to mention the music and movie industries' emphasis on self-aware-ness, self-gratification, and self-sufficiency. This fuels questioning of the Bible's authority. As the Lord's Day approaches, average church members' minds have been conditioned to question authority. Come Sunday morning, they sit before the preacher, the man of God, the one chosen to openly pro-claim, "Thus saith the Lord." Yet biblical illiteracy combined with postmodern inundation leaves some questioning whether what they heard was from God or from man.

Is It Black and White or Gray All Over?

Interestingly, postmodernism does not rule out religion altogether. In fact, people are encouraged to believe and embrace whatever teaching or ideol-ogy bests suits them. Postmodernism promotes religion cafeteria style. People choose what they want and what they don't want.

Postmodernism's rejection of absolute truth has caused even some evan-gelicals to question or reject long-held Christian convictions. Since, according to the postmodernist, what is right for one group is not necessarily right for everyone, the whole concept of biblical commands becomes problematic. If there are not absolute truths, the commands in Scripture should not be taken seriously. The Bible becomes a book full of "gray areas."

CONTEXTUALIZATION: THE POLE CONNECTOR

The Bible comes from an ancient Near Eastern culture, background, and environment that we have not experienced. The New Testament, for exam-ple, is a first-century book written in a language not familiar to the majority of Christians. There exists a chasm between the ancient biblical text and the world in which we presently live. The question at hand is, "How can Bible expositors bridge that chasm?"

Most Bible expositors agree that a sermon has two poles: the past meaning of the text and the present application of the text. Biblical preaching must draw from what the text meant to the original readers in order to apply that meaning to the contemporary audience. How does a preacher connect the two poles? The answer to that question is "contextualization."

Defining Contextualization

Contextualization, also known as "bridge building," ensures that God's Word speaks as clearly today as it did in ancient times. Some expositors refer to this as correlation, paradigm shifting, parallelism, or comparability.

Grant Osborne defines contextualization as "that dynamic process which interprets the significance of a religion or cultural norm for a group with a different cultural heritage."[4] This definition suggests that contextualization is identical to what many Bible preachers refer to as application. It is taking the content of unchanging biblical revelation and presenting it in a form applicable to the contemporary audience.[5] Jerry Vines refers to this process as determining the proposition of the sermon. He says, "This is where the expositor is intent upon moving from the then to the now without losing the Holy Spirit's intended meaning."[6] Harold Bryson prefers the phrase "bridge-building from text to people."[7] Professor Roy Zuck of Dallas Theological Seminary calls contextualization "bridging the cultural, grammatical and literary gaps."[8] Ramesh Richard prefers the term "contemporarization"[9] while John Stott speaks of "bridge-building."[10] Regardless of the terminology one uses, the objective is the same. William D. Thompson states that "while writers on interpretation use various terms for bridge building, their pursuit remains the same, moving from the past to the present."[11]

Contextualization is a matter of fusing the biblical and contemporary worlds together into one. It is seeking to match the biblical message to the contemporary situation. Osborne suggests a six-stage process of contextualization.[12] This process gradually moves from the biblical text to the modern context, and from the original meaning to the current significance. The overall intent of this process is to enable the church in diverse cultures to affirm and live out biblical truths with the same dynamic power as did the early church.[13]

Bridging the gap between the ancient world of the biblical text and the contemporary world requires sound exegesis, proper hermeneutics, and adequate

---

[4] Grant R. Osborne, *The Hermeneutical Spiral* (Downers Grove, IL: InterVarsity, 1991), 318.

[5] Ibid.

[6] Jerry Vines and Jim Shaddix, *Power in the Pulpit* (Chicago, IL: Moody, 2009), 135.

[7] Harold T. Bryson, *Expository Preaching: The Art of Preaching Through a Book of the Bible* (Nashville, TN: Broadman & Holman, 1995), 198.

[8] Roy B. Zuck, *Basic Bible Interpretation* (Grand Rapids, MI: Victor, 1991), 19.

[9] Ramesh Richard, *Preparing Expository Sermons* (Grand Rapids, MI: Baker, 2001), 19.

[10] Stott, *Between Two Worlds*, 135.

[11] William D. Thompson, *Preaching Biblically: Exegesis and Interpretation* (Nashville, TN: Abingdon, 1981), 51.

[12] Osborne, *The Hermeneutical Spiral*, 336–38. Osborne's six-stage process moves from what the text meant to what the text means. He evaluates the surface meaning of the text through exegesis. Here, the specific context is realized. He then proceeds to determine the deep structural principle through biblical theology. It is here that the general context is realized. Finally, he determines the original situation through background study. The overall design of this stage is to determine the parallel situation in the modern context.

[13] Ibid., 336.

application. The Bible preacher must study the meaning of the text to determine what God said to the ancient audience. The preacher then proclaims the text's significance for his contemporary audience. Throughout the process he never negates nor negotiates the original meaning. His ultimate quest is to move from the *then* to the *now* without losing the original intended meaning.

Demonstrating Contextualization

African American preaching is contextualized preaching. It seeks to merge what the Bible says into the current life situations of people. It's what black preachers call "identifying with the Scriptures."[14] When the preacher personally identifies with the Bible, his preaching meets the needs of those to whom he preaches. Listeners get a real sense of walking, talking, and living the text themselves. Bible truth becomes more than something theoretical, intended for the theological classroom only. Truth becomes something to experience, something to flesh out, and something to live.

Contextualization and "Eyewitness" Account Preaching

Henry Mitchell has coined the phrase "eyewitness account preaching"[15] to describe his process of contextualization. As the preacher engages in hermeneutics, he internalizes the teaching of the text and becomes an eyewitness reporter, perhaps one of several characters involved in the text. Eyewitnesses describe settings that are vivid and familiar. Listeners quickly visualize the picture and relate it to their situations. As Warren Stewart observes,

> As an eyewitness reporter an empathetic application of the text is carried out by the interpreter. He becomes a member of the Hebrew children in Egypt or Elijah battling the prophets of Baal or Jacob wrestling with an angel or the demoniac roaming the Gergesene country or Pilate washing his hands of Jesus' sentence or Paul struggling with his old nature or any other character who arises from a passage of Scripture.[16]

The result of identifying with the Bible as an eyewitness allows listeners to see that the text written centuries ago, can apply to their lives today. They become eyewitnesses themselves, and application becomes natural. Stewart

---

[14] Warren H. Stewart, Sr., *Interpreting God's Word in Black Preaching* (Valley Forge, PA: Judson, 1984), 30.

[15] Henry H. Mitchell, *Black Preaching: The Recovery of a Powerful Art* (Nashville, TN: Abingdon, 1990), 30.

[16] Stewart, *Interpreting God's Word in Black Preaching*, 30.

observes: "Moreover it should be noted that the preacher must be able to transmit this eyewitness account experience to those to whom his message is directed in order that they, too, can engage in empathetic application of the text."[17]

The African American community hungers for preaching that does more than stimulate the intellect. This is not to suggest black preaching should lack depth of biblical content. Rather it suggests that African American Christians long for teaching that personally impacts their lives. It is great to be able to identify theological terminology, note various dispensations in God's plan for the world, or argue in favor of a pre-tribulation rapture. But truth alone is not a sermon. Truth needs to be contextualized. The textual gap between the *then* and the *now* needs to be bridged and its two poles connected.

For the average black person living in the United States, daily life is full of disappointments, setbacks, and struggles. Poverty, unemployment, under-employment, single parenting, drugs, crime, and gang violence seem to be the foundation upon which most of urban America's communities are built. It is during the preaching event that biblical truths become personal mirrors as listeners see themselves and their situations more clearly. Encouragement is given to them as hope inspires them to continue their pursuit of knowing, loving, and more importantly obeying God.

Illustrating "Eyewitness" Account Preaching

In the black preaching tradition, contextualization is called "preaching in a common tongue."[18] This is preaching that communicates God's Word with cultural awareness and sensitivity.

One illustration of eyewitness account preaching is the classic sermon by Samuel D. Proctor, "Everybody Is God's Somebody," based on Acts 17:19–28.[19] Proctor sets the stage for his sermon by emphasizing the historical significance of the text. He takes his listeners on a mental trip back in time to first-century Athens, the educational and cultural center of the world during that time. It was a city that boasted of great philosophers. Proctor emphasizes

---

[17] Ibid., 31.

[18] Ibid., 53.

[19] Samuel D. Proctor and William D. Whatley, *Sermons from The Black Pulpit* (Valley Forge, PSA: Judson Press, 1984), 25–33. The late Dr. Samuel D. Proctor served as pastor of the historic Abyssinian Baptist Church in New York City. He also served as professor of the practice of Christian ministry at Duke Divinity School, and professor emeritus at The Graduate School of Education, Rutgers University.

that Athens was a town filled with statues, street lecturers, religious teachers, and intellectual groups such as the Stoics, Epicureans, and Hedonists.[20]

It is at this point that Proctor introduces his listeners to a very special individual from the text. That individual is the apostle Paul. Proctor says, "To this Athens now came a Jewish tentmaker from Tarsus, short, baldheaded, a Roman citizen, and student of Gamaliel, preaching that Jesus is the Son of God."[21] As he and his listeners visualize themselves in Athens, Proctor stresses that Paul, seemingly uneducated in the minds of philosophers, was given the task of lecturing the audience. The Athenians were accustomed to new personalities coming through their city looking for followers. They also allowed time for these visitors to gain their own following. Proctor says, "So Paul was given the same license as everyone else. They interviewed him, 'What is this new doctrine you speak of?' Paul must have answered them sufficiently for they set a date for him to have his say on Mars Hill, an open lecture area where the philosophers always spoke."[22]

Proctor's message now begins to shift from the *then* to the *now*. This is the moment of contextualization. The preacher tells his listeners what he believes was Paul's purpose in traveling to Athens:

> Paul served notice. He did not come there to organize a small following. He came there to tell them that the whole human race was one, that one God has made all people, and that in Christ God was bringing this whole human family together to a knowledge of himself. In other words, in Christ everybody is somebody.[23]

Proctor's sermon focuses on the current need of his listeners to obey God's will. Such obedience involves treating all humanity as children of God regardless of race, creed, or color. Proctor's message conveys that the outstanding feature of the life and teaching of Jesus Christ is that he reached beyond his own people and shed abroad the love of God in the lives of all people. Proctor adds, "Jesus treated all persons as though they were all God's children."[24]

To contextualize his selected text, Proctor takes his listeners on another mental journey. They now travel from New Testament Greece to the United States, a nation engulfed with segregation, racism, and bigotry. He reminds listeners of the decades when black people suffered constant insults and abuses

---

[20] Ibid., 26.
[21] Ibid.
[22] Ibid.
[23] Ibid.
[24] Ibid.

that were intended to destroy their pride and self-respect. He then encourages his listeners by bringing to their minds the truth that black people have a history of praying their way through challenging situations.

Proctor's message concludes with excitement and hope for individuals, the nation, and the entire world:

> Finally, in a positive sense, when we believe that God has made us all one blood, that belief becomes the foundation for the building of a true, genuine, and lasting community among all people, one that rises above race and clan, one that extends beyond tongue and nation, one that embraces the whole human family. Such a community comes about in the hearts and minds of persons and cannot be created by government or established by decree. It cannot be established by the state or denied by the state. Its charter is what Paul proclaimed in Athens, *"God has made of one blood all nations. . . ."*[25]

Proctor's sermon is a good example of contextualized preaching. With his unique style, oratory skills, and use of colorful language, he was able to take New Testament realities and merge them into his contemporary culture. He painted a mental picture of the scene in first-century Athens. He taught what he believed to be the significance of that scene. He then led his listeners out of the first century back into their present situation. It was at this point that the two poles were connected. The gap between the ancient text and contemporary situation was bridged. The listeners were encouraged to "rebuild their attitudes, redesign strategies, redefine their goals, and reorder their priorities"[26] to conform to the will of God.[27]

A Potential Danger of Eyewitness Account Preaching

One potential danger this writer sees with "eyewitness account" preaching is that it may obscure the original meaning of a text in the name of contemporary application. Proctor's message is illustrative in that he failed to underscore the true intent of the text. It is true that God has made one race out of all human beings. It is equally true that humans are to treat everyone with dignity and respect. After all, God has created us all. However, that reality is of secondary importance in the text compared with Paul's call for the Athenians to receive Jesus Christ as their personal Lord and Savior. Paul proclaimed:

[25] Ibid., 31.
[26] Ibid., 33.
[27] Other examples of eyewitness account preaching are noted in Darryl D. Sims, ed., *Sound the Trumpet: Messages to Empower African-American Men* (Valley Forge, PA: Judson, 2002).

> And the times of this ignorance God winked at; but now comman-
> deth all men everywhere to repent: Because he hath appointed a day,
> in the which he will judge the world in righteousness by that man
> whom he hath ordained; whereof he hath given assurance unto all
> men, in that he hath raised him from the dead. (Acts 17:30–31)

Though meaningful in rallying his listeners to demonstrate respect to all people, Proctor's message failed to highlight the more serious subject of sin and salvation. This subject was foremost in Paul's mind and that of Luke—the author of Acts. This is evidenced by the text's ending. Having mentioned the coming judgment of God and the death and resurrection of his Son Jesus Christ, the text concludes by noting what took place as Paul departed from Athens: "Howbeit certain men clave unto him and believed: among the which was Dionysius the Areopagite, and a woman named Damaris, and others with them" (Acts 17:34).

If the preacher's focus is merely to become an "eyewitness," he may be tempted to ignore the theological intent of the passage. When that happens, the Bible is made to say something other than its intended meaning. When the Bible is treated as a book for personal identification alone, the preacher's personal opinions and biases can obscure the meaning. Also, the theological implications are blurred and not synched with the application. Such preaching has given rise to teachings like black liberation theology, the social gospel, and prosperity theology.

PERSPECTIVES ON EFFECTIVELY COMMUNICATING GOD'S WORD

To conclude our discussion of relevance in biblical preaching, it may be helpful to examine the perspectives of five seasoned pulpiteers—three African American and two white.[28] These men were selected based on their training and tenure of service in Christian ministry. None is a novice. Each has been preaching for many years, and each preaches regularly in his local church.

Following are the six questions posed to each of the five preachers along with their responses. The preachers interviewed are Bruce H. Anderson, pastor of Olivet Baptist Church in Westwood, Kansas; John Clayton, pastor of Willington Baptist Temple in Wellington, Kansas; Erskine Dodson, pastor of Trinity Baptist Church in Indianapolis, Indiana; Kevin James Lavender Sr. (younger brother of the author), pastor of Bible Baptist Church in Kalamazoo,

---

[28] See Appendix A for the complete list of preachers selected for the interview.

Michigan; and Antoine Richardson, president of the Carver Baptist Bible College and Theological Seminary in Kansas City, Missouri.

What Preaching Method Do You Prefer, and Why?

Anderson: Most often I preach expositionally with a verse-by-verse approach. I also will preach topically or do a survey of a given book. The reason I prefer an expositional approach is that God uses his Word to convict and change lives (cf. Heb 4:12; 1 Pet 1:23–25).

Clayton: I am almost totally committed to biblical exposition. Sometimes this takes the form of preaching through an entire book (example: I am presently preaching through Acts), sometimes a significant part of a book (example: the Sermon on the Mount), and sometimes a series of doctrinal or practical messages based on key biblical passages (example: this year during advent I am preaching on the incarnation using New Testament passages which speak of the Son "becoming" as in John 1:1–18 and 2 Cor 8:9).

Dodson: I use an expositional approach to study and preaching of the Word of God. It will often be verse-by-verse and book studies. There are times I use a topical study, but I also believe topical study should still be exegetically prepared and preached.

Lavender: I prefer the expositional and narrative methods of preaching. My preference is based upon the natural presentation of the biblical text. As I humbly communicate God's message to his people in the pew, I find that biblical exposition allows me to present the thoughts and build on them in the order that the biblical writer received them. Also, I find that through exposition I can deal with each subject as it is presented in the text. When I have preached topical messages, I have tended to stay away from subjects that I personally may be struggling with in my life. I find that the topic oftentimes will dictate to the biblical text. With exposition, the message presented comes from the text.

Richardson: The preaching method I utilize most frequently is expository in nature. I believe it is important to make the meaning of the text plain to the hearer so that they may understand his mind regarding the text (Neh 8:8). We also are able to get a better understanding of the text as we relate it to the immediate and remote context of the surrounding Scriptures.

Why Is Preaching Important to You?

Anderson: Preaching is important because God has ordained to bless his Word and the proclamation of it (cf. 1 Cor 1:17–21), and because the Lord has called me to preach his Word (cf. 1 Cor 9:16, 23; Col. 4:17).

Clayton: A first practical reason is my own experience. God used preaching to bring me to salvation. Preaching was one of the major things that contributed to my growth as a Christian and to my love for the Lord Jesus Christ. Theologically, preaching is important because it is by the "foolishness of preaching" (1 Cor 1:18–21) that God has chosen to "save them that believe." To faithfully fulfill the ministry of pastoral preaching one must, as Paul did in Ephesus, declare "the whole counsel of God" (Acts 20:27).

Dodson: It's important because God has ordained it to be the number one priority when it comes to the pastor's ministry (cf. 2 Tim 4:1–3). It is also important because the only way one can get saved is through preaching of the gospel of Jesus Christ (cf. Rom 10:17). As they come to Christ, people need to be equipped to do the work of ministry. This also comes by the preaching of God's Word (cf. Eph 4:11–12). Finally, the Word of God is the only thing we have that gives us the direction to navigate ourselves in life. Apart from God's Word, one will be left to their own understanding without a biblical compass in this dispensation of time. Without the Word being lived out, one's life will end up shipwrecked.

Lavender: Preaching is important to me because God has chosen preaching as one of the primary ways to disclose his Word to the world (Titus 1:2–3). Preaching also provides the opportunity for people to get to know God in a deeper way, allowing for a more meaningful worship of God in truth.

Richardson: God's people long to hear a word from him while God longs to communicate with his people. Biblical preaching allows God's people as well as the non-believer to respond to him based on truth. The preached word instructs, reproves, corrects, and trains the believer to be equipped to 1) live in a way that is pleasing to God and 2) make disciples. Those who are called to preach have been charged by God to clearly communicate the unadulterated Word of God to his people.

What Role Does Exegetical Study Play in Your Sermon Preparation?

Anderson: Exegetical study is the first thing I do in sermon preparation. I want to be true to God's Word. I need to know what it says before I apply what it says to me (cf. 1 Cor 1:17; 2:2).

Clayton: Exegetical study is my starting point. My goal is to let the text speak. Therefore, my first goal is to know what the text says. My conviction is that our first goal is to determine authorial intent. Most of the time, the exegetical details that are carefully worked out in the study will be left there. To bring them to the pulpit would be telling people more than they want to know. I should add here that to be an effective expositor of the Scriptures, one should engage in serious and regular biblical exegesis. I would add to this my conviction that there is a biblical theology. The thing that impresses me most about the Scriptures is the inter-relatedness of all Scripture. There are several contexts into which every text that we preach must be placed: its context within the specific passage where it is found, its context within the book in which it is found, its context within the writings of its author, etc. But the more you see each text within the context of the entire biblical revelation, the richer your preaching will be.

Dodson: Exegesis plays a major role in my sermon preparation. Exegesis means to lead out; to pull out the true and original meaning of the text. Without good sound exegesis, one would put their own opinions and meanings on the text, which always leads to a human philosophy or teaching. That would of course lead to a human lifestyle that's contrary to God and his Word.

Lavender: In sermon preparation there is a bridge that preachers must cross. Exegetical study allows me to cross the bridge of the great gulf that exists between the writer's mind and my mind. By crossing the bridge through study, I am able to get to the mind, language, and culture in which the writings occurred.

Richardson: I believe that exegetical study of the text is critical to ensuring first of all that I understand what God is saying and intends to communicate through the text. I believe a text only has one meaning intended by the ultimate author, God. Our job is to utilize hermeneutical principles to discover the meaning of the text and relate the application(s) to the hearer (Neh 8:8). I recognize that exegetical study takes time and effort, however, I believe it is critical to good sermon preparation.

Much Is Said Today about "Relevant Preaching." What Are Your Thoughts on This Topic?

Anderson: God's Word is always "relevant," meeting the needs of lost mankind and bringing them into conformity to the image of Christ (Rom 8:29; 12:2; Phil 3:10). Man does not always understand his need. Therefore, it is important to understand culture and help each one come to grips with Christ's claim on them (1 Cor 9:19–23; 10:32–33). Though we may alter our approach in different settings, the message is the eternal Word of God and must not be altered to conform to the world's expectations (1 Pet 1:23).

Clayton: My goal is to let the text speak, not to find a text that speaks to a particular current situation or topic. I am convinced that if individuals are growing strong in Christ, if they are being "renewed in the spirit of their minds" (Eph 4:23), then they will be equipped to deal with life. God's truth is timeless and human nature is constant, so the Bible is never irrelevant. Currently the most pressing problem of preaching is not the relevancy of Scripture, but ignorance of Scripture. We can no longer assume that those who attend church somewhat regularly have an even elementary understanding of Scripture and of basic Christian teachings. Our goal is to help people see that the fundamental problem of life is sin.

Dodson: We are called to preach the Word of God. The Word of God itself is relevant, it is "forever . . . settled in heaven" (Ps 119:89). You cannot add anything to it or take anything away from it. As one preaches the pure unadulterated Word of God, it is important to use illustrations that are relevant in the sense that people can relate to your illustrations. It is also important to make proper application of the text to your audience.

Lavender: I believe that all true preaching must achieve two objectives in order to be effective. First, we must get back to the mind of the writer of Scripture, bridging the gap between the writer's mind and my mind. Second, we must take in consideration the mind of the people in our churches today. There must be prayerful presentation of the message of Scripture and how it speaks, and its application to current issues. The utmost care and caution should be exercised by the preacher in any attempts to try to "make the Bible relevant." Such attempts may violate the warning not to add or take away from the Word of God. The Bible was given to us from an eternal perspective. From the view of God, everything is always present tense.

Richardson: I am not intimately familiar with how others are using the term "relevant preaching." However, any preaching that attempts to be relevant without searching the Scripture in a systematic way to find out God's mind about the subject is of little use to the hearer. Instead, the preacher, as a part of his exegetical study, must build a "hermeneutical bridge" to ensure that the listener has the best chance of understanding the relevance of the text to his/her life. Jesus often did this, relating the unfamiliar to that which was familiar to the hearer.

What Is Postmodernism and How Has Your Preaching Been Affected by It?

Anderson: Postmodernism is usually understood as the rejection of absolutes and objective reality. It values personal reality and is skeptical of all who profess to know the absolute truth for everyone else. Truth is relative for each individual. Experience is more significant than abstract constructs of morality. The Bible has much to say that is relevant to postmodernism. Man has always been self-absorbed in one way or another and desired to "be as gods" (Gen 3:5). I need to be aware of how thinking has changed and confront the skeptic with the truth. The Word of God can change cultural conditioning (Titus 1:9–14).

Clayton: We could start with Jean-Francois Lyotard's definition of postmodernism as the absence of meta-narratives. If this is true, then the Christian or Judeo-Christian worldview that has guided Western culture for centuries can no longer be considered predominant. Many would say we can no longer consider it to be universally true (hence no more Ten Commandments on courthouse walls), but only of use to those who embrace it. Some of the effects of this for preaching are: we must not assume that even Christians believe in truth with a capital T; a second consequence is the heightened need for civility of discourse in preaching and in all that we say. We must learn to argue like Christians; third, one particularly positive consequence is that postmodernism should force us to try harder to understand those who are not like us. We must be very careful that in opposing error we understand what we are opposing and that we always treat people who oppose us with dignity and grace; finally, in the end our role has not changed. We are to bear witness to Jesus Christ in the power of the Holy Spirit.

Dodson: Postmodernism means everything is relative. There are no absolutes. A postmodernist believes what's good and right is based on the individual or situation, not the Word of God, and each person decides what's good for them. It's based upon man's feelings and intellect independently of the Scriptures. This belief can change from one belief to another, all based upon the way one thinks or feels at the time. One whose faith is based and anchored on the Word of God believes that in spite of changes in culture or current thinking, they will rest their faith and practice on the unchangeable Word of God.

Lavender: Britannica defines postmodernism as a late twentieth-century movement characterized by broad skepticism, subjectivism, or relativism; a general suspicion of reason; and an acute sensitivity to the role of ideology in asserting and maintaining political and economic power. My personal view is that postmodernism is simply philosophical and sociological Darwinism. The idea that man is evolving and progressing apart from any need for God. This supposed move upward is really a fast move downward. I continue to preach the Word of God from belief in the authority, infallibility, and inerrancy of the biblical text.

Richardson: In a nutshell, postmodernism holds that there is no objective truth and that morality is relative (objective truth vs. relative truth). There is a very prevalent misconception in today's society that "what might be right for you may not be right for me." Postmodern views have provided me with even more passion to reach others with the truth of the gospel, especially those of a younger generation. I have been compelled to study the Word of God, which provides absolute truth, to relate it to the arguments that people are attempting to use to support their belief in "a number of truths." It has been rewarding to see lives changed, especially of young people as they attempt fruitlessly to refute the authority and authenticity of the Bible. It in turn has strengthened their belief in the Bible as they make honest attempts to challenge its authority.

Explain What Part the Listener Has in the Preaching Event

Anderson: I must endeavor to reach the minds and hearts of those listening (Col 4:3–6). However, only God can open their hearts and bring conviction (1 Cor 1:18; 2:4–5, 11–14; 3:6–7). I need to encourage them to personally apply the Word of God to their lives (Jas 1:21–25). Congregational enthusiasm and verbal response may or may not indicate personal application of the message.

Clayton: Let me begin by saying we preach to real people. No two are quite alike, and we have a responsibility to all. We cannot preach to people without knowing people. One of the great advantages of pastoral ministry is that we preach to the same people regularly. We have ample opportunity to know them. The pastor lives in two worlds, the world of the Word of God, and the world of his congregation. It is his job to take the light of the first to help make sense out of the second. He starts with himself. The text must speak to the preacher before it can speak to the congregation. He must then visualize how it will be received.

Dodson: The listener has the responsibility to make sure what they hear is filtered through the Word of God, and they must make proper and personal application to their lives so that they will not be just hearers, but doers also.

Lavender: As listeners of preaching, we have the responsibility of hearing and obeying what we hear. Not as the words of men, but of God. We should also express our agreement ("Amen") with what we hear. Double honor should be given the preacher who labors in doctrine. There should also be a demonstration of the working power of the Holy Spirit through the Word of God through the change of life. And finally, the things that we hear we are responsible to teach to others who are faithful.

Richardson: The listener has (at least) the following responsibilities: Carefully examine the Scriptures (like the Bereans) to ensure that what is being taught lines up with the Word of God (Acts 17:11). Allow Scripture to equip them for every good work (2 Tim 3:16–17). This includes correction and reproof. Allow the Spirit of God to convict the hearer of sin (John 16:8). Be prepared to put the Word of God into practice (Jas 1:22).

Personal Observation

Given the racial and cultural makeup of the interviewees, one might expect their answers to express very different views. Quite the contrary! Each was in total agreement on the foundational principles of Bible study, exegesis, and interpretation. The difference between their views occurred mainly in the realm of their approach to exposition. Each contributor stressed the importance of bridging the gap between the ancient world of the biblical text and the contemporary world.

ACCOMMODATION VERSUS EXPOSITION

Scott Gibson aptly notes the need for relevance in biblical preaching:

> The church itself has accommodated to the culture in subtle and not so subtle ways. Sermons have become antidotes to bruised egos, lists of how-to's, and topical discussions on any number of themes—but not biblically centered expositions of what the Bible said to the people and the culture to which it was written and what it says to men and women today.[29]

In this chapter the relevance of biblical preaching was studied. Three topics were discussed to reveal the importance of relevant preaching.

The first topic discussed was postmodernism and its effect of biblical preaching. Postmodernism was defined as the philosophy of life that believes absolute truth does not exist. It holds that all belief systems are valid and no one system is of greater value than others. Postmodernism's emphasis on tolerance, individualism, and moral relativism has created a culture where the authority of God's Word is readily questioned.

---

[29] Scott M. Gibson, ed., *Preaching to a Shifting Culture* (Grand Rapids, MI: Baker, 2004), 221.

The second topic studied was contextualization. Contextualization bridges the gap between the ancient world of the biblical text and the contemporary world. It was determined that sound exegesis, proper hermeneutics, and adequate application of God's Word are necessary for affective contextualization. "Eyewitness" account preaching was presented as an example of contextualization.

The third topic discussed was gaining the proper perspective for effective Bible proclamation. Interviews were conducted with a cross section of preachers on this topic, with six questions posed to each preacher.

DISCUSSION QUESTIONS

1. What evidence is there that God's Word accomplishes what he intends for it to accomplish?
2. What effect has postmodernism had on biblical preaching?
3. What is the basic philosophy of postmodernism?
4. In your own words, explain the struggle between postmodernism and absolute truth.
5. Define contextualization and explain why it is considered a pole connector.
6. Define "eyewitness account" preaching and explain its strengths and weaknesses.

Conclusion

THE purpose of this conclusion is not only to bring this study to a close but also to highlight the important issues that have been presented. It was the objective of this book to underscore the importance of accurate and relevant preaching in African American pulpits.

In chapter one, the need for restoration of biblical accuracy and relevance was addressed. The crisis facing African American churches was traced to three primary influences: the social gospel, black liberation theology, and the prosperity gospel. All three have distorted the true gospel message.

In chapter two, the importance of biblical exegesis was explored. This discussion was premised on the reality that some preachers have abandoned the belief that the Bible is God's final authority to men. Sound exegesis was presented as the means to safeguard against misrepresenting the biblical text. The disciplines of Bible introduction, hermeneutics, and biblical languages were presented as tools needed for biblical exegesis.

In chapter three, a theology of preaching was discussed. God is the originator of preaching, and therefore all preachers are commissioned to communicate his Word. Within the context of this principle, the nature of biblical preaching and the ethos of preaching in the African American context were studied. The importance and value of expository preaching was also analyzed. It was determined that while all preaching methods have value, the expository method best carries out the biblical admonition to "preach the word."

In chapter four, relevance in biblical preaching was examined. Postmodernism and its effect on biblical preaching was analyzed. In addition, interviews with seasoned Bible preachers were conducted on effectively communicating God's Word. Postmodernism was defined as a philosophy or worldview that says absolute truth does not exist. This has affected biblical preaching. Countless people sit before God's Word each Lord's Day and end up questioning the Bible's authority.

This study made one truth particularly clear: African American pulpits are in desperate need of a spiritual makeover. It is incumbent upon black preachers to fulfill their calling to preach God's Word because most problems faced by the black community relate to its deficiencies in understanding the Bible. As Thabiti Anyabwile aptly comments,

> Most theological difficulties stem from root deficiencies in comprehending the nature and content of the Bible. Though African-Americans are predominantly evangelical in their attitudes toward the Bible—that is, we believe it to be the "Word of God" in some sense—we are no longer centered upon the Bible in faith and practice.[1]

Today more than ever, biblical accuracy and relevance need to be restored to preaching. The reasons for this are too numerous to expound in this work. There is one reason, however, that supersedes all others: the need for changed lives. Biblical preaching effects changes in the lives of its listeners. The road from salvation to spiritual maturity is paved with biblical preaching. The people of God come together each Lord's Day not to be entertained. They come to be fed a full diet of Scripture. They come expecting their pastor to communicate to God's Word to them. They come asking the question, "Is there a word from the Lord?"

The preaching from African American pulpits should be the high point of the worship service. Good fellowship and enthusiastic singing should merely set the tone for the main event of preaching. As he stands to read, explain, and expound God's Word, the preacher should be confident he has done an adequate job of exegeting, interpreting, and contextualizing the biblical text. All of his personal biases, opinions, and presuppositions must be left behind. He enters his pulpit with God's words on his mind and in his heart. He stands ready to proclaim a Word other than his own. As he opens his mouth to preach, the Holy Spirit reminds him of Paul's admonition to Pastor Timothy,

---

[1] Thabiti M. Anyabwile, *The Decline of African-American Theology* (Downers Grove, IL: InterVarsity, 2007), 241.

> I charge thee therefore before God, and the Lord Jesus Christ, who shall judge the quick and the dead at his appearing and his kingdom; Preach the word; be instant in season, out of season; reprove, rebuke, exhort with all longsuffering and doctrine. For the time will come when they will not endure sound doctrine; but after their own lusts shall they heap to themselves teachers, having itching ears; And they shall turn away their ears from the truth, and shall be turned unto fables. But watch thou in all things, endure afflictions, do the work of an evangelist, make full proof of thy ministry. (2 Tim 4:1–5)

These challenging words should be etched in the mind and on the heart of every preacher. This is the burden of preaching. The preaching burden is perhaps what Paul had in mind when he said to the Corinthian Church, "for necessity is laid upon me; yea, woe is unto me, if I preach not the gospel!" (1 Cor 9:16).

Paul was compelled to preach the gospel of Jesus Christ and dreaded the prospect of shirking his responsibility. He believed that a most painful and tragic result would ensue in his life if he did not in fact preach the gospel.[2] Indeed, any man who claims his calling as a preacher of God's Word and yet fails to preach it accurately should expect painful and tragic results.

---

[2] Paige Patterson, *The Troubled Triumphant Church: An Exposition of First Corinthians* (Nashville, TN: Thomas Nelson, 1983), 147.

Bibliography

Adams, Jay E. *Preaching with Purpose: The Urgent Task of Homiletics.* Grand Rapids, MI: Zondervan, 1982.

Andrews, Dale P. *Practical Theology for Black Churches: Bridging Black Theology and African Amerian Folk Religion.* Louisville, KY: Westminster John Knox, 2002.

Andrews, Sherry. "Keping the Faith." *Charisma,* 1981.

Anyabwile, Thabiti M. *The Decline of African-American Theology: From Biblical Faith to Cultural Captivity.* Downer's Grove, IL: InterVarsity, 2007.

Azurdia, Arturo G., III. *Spirit Empowered Preaching.* Great Britain: Christian Focus, 2003.

Baldwin, Lewis V. "Black Christianity in the South in the Nineteenth Century: Its Development and Character." *Religion in the South Conference Papers.* Birmingham, AL: Alabama Humanities Foundation, 1986.

Banks, William L. *The History of Black Baptists in the United States.* Philadelphia, PA: The Continental Press, 1987.

Berkley, James D. *Leadership Handbook of Preaching and Worship: Practical Insight from a Cross Section of Ministry Leaders.* Grand Rapids, MI: Baker, 1992.

Bowens, Jeffery B. *Prosperity Gospel: Prosperity Gospel and Its Effect on the 21st Century Church.* Bloomington, IL: Xlibris, 2012.

Bryson, Harold T. *Expository Preaching: The Art of Preaching Through a Book of the Bible.* Nashville, TN: Broadman & Holman, 1995.

Carson, Clayborne, ed. *The Autobiography of Martin Luther King Jr.* New York, NY: Grand Central, 1998.

Cleage, Albert B., Jr. *The Black Messiah.* New York, NY: Sheed and Ward, 1968.

Cone, James. *A Black Theology of Liberation.* Maryknoll, NY: Orbis, 1990.

Copan, Paul. *That's Just Your Interpretation.* Grand Rapids, MI: Baker, 2001.

Copeland, Kenneth. *The Troublemaker.* Forth Worth, TX: Copeland Ministries, 1970.

Draper, James T., Jr., and Kenneth Keathley. *Biblical Authority: The Critical Issue for the Body of Christ.* Nashville, TN: Broadman & Holman Publishers, 2001.

Farmer, Ronald L. *Beyond the Impasse: The Promise of a Process Hermeneutic.* Atlanta, GA: Mercer University Press, 1977.

Fee, Gordon D. *Listening to the Spirit in the Text.* Grand Rapids, MI: Wm. B. Eerdmans, 2000.

———. *New Testament Exegesis.* Louisville, KY: Wesminster John Knox, 1983.

Franklin, John Hope. *From Slavery to Freedom:A History of Negro Americans.* New York, NY: Alfred A. Knopf, 1974.

Frazier, E. Franklin. *The Negro Church in America.* New York, NY: Schocken, 1963.

Gibson, Scott M., ed. *Preaching to a Shifting Culture.* Grand Rapids, MI: Baker, 2004.

Gilbert, Larry. *Team Ministry: A Guide to Spiritual Gifts and Lay Involvement.* Lynchburg, VA: Church Growth Institute, 1989.

Greidanus, Sidney. *The Modern Preaher and the Ancient Text: Interpreting and Preaching Biblical Literature.* Grand Rapids, MI: Eerdmans, 1988.

Gromacki, Robert G. *Stand True to the Charge: An Exposition of 1 Timothy.* Schaumburg, IL: Regular Baptist Press, 1982.

Hagin, Kenneth. *Redeemed from Poverty, Sickness, and Spiritual Death.* Tulsa, OK: Rhema Bible Church, 1997.

Hamilton, Charles V. *The Black Preacher in America.* New York, NY: William Morrow & Company, 1972.

Hanegraff, Hank. *Christianity in Crisis.* Eugene, OR: Harvest House, 1993.

Harris, James H. *Preaching Liberation.* Minneapolis, MN: Augsburg, 1995.

Hinn, Benny. *Rise and Be Healed.* Orlando, FL: Celebration, 1991.

Jakes, T. D. *Life Overflowing: 6 Pillars for Abundant Living.* Minneapolis, MN: Bethany House, 2008.

Johnston, Graham. *Preaching to a Postmodern World: A Guide to Reaching Twenty-First Century Listeners.* Grand Rapids, MI: Baker, 2001.

Kaiser, Walter C., Jr. *Toward An Exegetical Theology:Biblical Exegesis for Preaching and Teaching.* Grand Rapids, MI: Baker, 1981.

Kaiser, Walter C., Jr., and Moisés Silva. *An Introduction to Biblical Hermeneutics.* Grand Rapids, MI: Zondervan, 1994.

Kent, Homer. *The Epistle to the Hebrews.* Grand Rapids, MI: Baker, 1972.

———. *The Pastoral Epistles: Studies in I nd II Timothy and Titus.* Chicago, IL: Moody, 1958.

LaRue, Cleophus J. *The Heart of Black Preaching.* Louisville, KY: Westminster John Knox, 2000.

LaRue, Cleophus J., ed. *More Power in the Pulpit:How America's Most Effective Black Preachers Prepare Their Sermons.* Louisville, KY: Westminster John Knox, 2009.

Lavender, Aaron. *Are You a Full Gospel Christian?* Maitland, FL: Xulon, 2007.

Loscalzo, Craig A. *Apologetic Preaching:Proclaiming Christ to a Postmodern World.* Downers Grove, IL: InterVarsity, 2000.

MacArthur, John, Jr. *Rediscovering Expository Preaching.* Dallas, TX: Word, 1995.

MacDonald, William, ed. *Believer's Bible Commentary.* Nashville, TN: Thomas Nelson, 1989.

McConnell, D. R. *A Different Gospel.* Peabody, MA: Hendrickson, 1995.

McElrath, Jessica. *The Everything Martin Luther King Jr. Book.* Avon, MA: Adams Media, 2008.

Mickelson, A. Berkeley. *Interpreting the Bible.* Grand Rapids, MI: Baker, 1981.

Miller, Donald G. *Fire in Thy Mouth.* 1954. Reprint, Grand Rapids, MI: Baker, 1976.

Mitchell, Henry H. *Black Preaching: The Recovery of a Powerful Art.* Nashville, TN: Abingdon, 1990.

Mohler, R. Albert, Jr. *He Is Not Silent: Preaching in a Postmodern World.* Chicago, IL: Moody, 2008.

Montoya, Alex. *Preaching with Passion.* Grand Rapids, MI: Kregel, 2000.

Moyd, Olin P. *The Sacred Art: Preaching and Theology in the African-American Tradition.* Valley Forge, PA: Judson, 1995.

Oden, Thomas C. *After Modernity . . . What? Agenda for Theology.* Grand Rapids, MI: Zondervan, 1990.

Olford, Stephen F. *Anointed Expository Preaching.* Nashville, TN: Broadman & Holman, 1998.

Osborne, Grant R. *The Hermeneutical Spiral*. Downers Grove, IL: InterVarsity, 1991.

Osborne, Linda Barrett. *Miles to Go for Freedom: Segregation and Civil Rights in the Jim Crow Years*. New York, NY: Abrams, 2012.

Paris, Peter J. *The Social Teachings of the Black Churches*. Philadelphia, PA: Fortress, 1985.

Patterson, Paige. *The Troubled Triumphant Church: An Exposition of First Corinthians*. Nashville, TN: Thomas Nelson, 1983.

Phillips, John. *Exploring the Minor Prophets: An Expository Commentary*. Grand Rapids, MI: Kregel, 1998.

———. *Exploring the Pastoral Epistles: An Expository Commentary*. Grand Rapids, MI: Kregel, 2004.

Piper, John. *The Supremacy of God in Preaching*. Grand Rapids, MI: Baker, 2004.

Poythress, Vern S., and Wayne A. Grudem. *The Gender-Neutral Bible Controversy: Muting the Masculinity of God's Word*. Nashville, TN: Broadman & Holman, 2000.

Proctor, Samuel D., and William D. Whatley. *Sermons from the Black Pulpit*. Valley Forge, PA: Judson, 1984.

Richard, Ramesh. *Preparing Expository Sermons*. Grand Rapids, MI: Baker, 2001.

Roberts, J. Deotis. *Africentric Christianity: A Theological Appraisal for Ministry*. Valley Forge, PA: Judson, 2000.

———. *The Prophethood of Black Believers: An African-American Political Theology for Ministry*. Louisville, KY: Westminster John Knox, 1994.

Robinson, Haddon W. *Biblical Preaching: The Development and Delivery of Expository Messages*. Grand Rapids, MI: Baker, 1980.

Robinson, Haddon W., and Torrey Robinson. *It's All in How You Tell It: Preparing First-Person Expository Messages*. Grand Rapids, MI: Baker, 2003.

Smith, Wallace Charles. *The Church in the Life of the Black Family*. Valley Forge, PA: Judson, 1985.

Stewart, Warren H. Sr. *Interpreting God's Word in Black Preaching*. Valley Forge, PA: Judson, 1984.

Stott, John. *Between Two Worlds: The Challenge of Preaching Today*. Grand Rapids, MI: Wm. B. Eerdmans, 1982.

Thiessen, Henry C. *Lectures in Systematic Theology*. Revised by Vernon D. Doerksen. Grand Rapids, MI: Wm. B. Eerdmans, Co, 1979.

Thomas, Frank A. *They Like to Never Quit Praisin' God: The Role of Celebration in Preaching*. Cleveland, OH: The Pilgrim Press, 1997.

Thomas, Robert L. *Ephesians Through Philemon*. Volume 11 of *The Expositor's Bible Commentary*. Frank E. Gaebelein, general editor. Grand Rapids, MI: Zondervan, 1981.

————. *Evangelical Hermeneutics:The New Versus the Old*. Grand Rapids, MI: Kregel, 2002.

Thompson, William D. *Preaching Biblically: Exegesis and Interpretation*. Nashville, TN: Abingdon, 1981.

Thurman, Howard. *Jesus and the Disinherited*. Boston, MA: Beacon, 1976.

Unger, Merrill F. *Unger's Commentary on the Old Testament*. Chattanooga, TN: AMG International, 2002.

Vine, W. E. *Vine's Complete Expository Dictionary of Old and New Testament Words*. Nashville, TN: Thomas Nelson, 1996.

Vines, Jerry, and Jim Shaddix. *Power in the Pulpit*. Chicago, IL: Moody, 1999.

Walls, David, and Max Anders. *1 & 2 Peter, 1, 2, & 3 John, Jude*. Holman New Testament Commentary. Nashville, TN: Broadman & Holman, 1999.

Walvoord, John F., and Roy B. Zuck, eds. *The Bible Knowledge Commentary: Old and New Testaments*. Colorado Springs, CO: David C. Cook, 1985.

Weber, Stuart K. *Matthew*. Holman New Testament Commentary. Nashville, TN: Broadman & Holman, 2000.

Webster's Ninth New Collegiate Dictionary. Springfield, MA: Merriam Webster, 1988.

West, Cornel. *Hope on a Tightrope*. New York, NY: Smiley, 2008.

Wiley, Ralph. *Why Black People Tend to Shout*. New York, NY: Penguin, 1991.

Willhite, Keith, and Scott M. Gibson. *The Big Idea of Biblical Preaching*. Grand Rapids, MI: Baker, 1998.

Zuck, Roy B. *Basic Bible Interpretation*. Grand Rapids, MI: Victor, 1991.

Appendix A
Examples of Contextualized Sermon Outlines

The following sermon outlines demonstrate faithfulness to the text while bridging the gap between the *then* and the *now*.

EXAMPLE NUMBER ONE

Sermon Title: Understanding What It Means to Be a Man
Sermon Text: Genesis 1:26–28; 2:7–9, 15
Introduction:

I. Being a Man Means We're Part of God's Plan: "Let us make man . . ." (Gen 1:26; see also 2:7)
   A. God created us men with hands-on care (2:7).
   B. God breathed into our nostrils his life (2:7).
II. Being a Man Means We're Part of God's Pattern: "So God created man in his own image . . ." (Gen 1:27)
   A. As God's image bearers we men are separated from the animal kingdom.
   B. As God's image bearers we men are able to know God personally.
   C. As God's image bearers we men have true significance and meaning in lie.
III. Being a Man Means We're Part of God's Purpose (Gen 2:8, 15)
   A. It is God's purpose for us men to work (2:15, "and put him in the garden of Eden to dress [tend] it").
   B. It is God's purpose for us men to protect and sustain ("to tend and keep it").

EXAMPLE NUMBER TWO

Sermon Title: Male and Female He Created Them
Sermon Text: Genesis 1:26–27
Introduction:

I. The Truth about Contemporary Gender Struggles

     A. Male chauvinism—the intentional disrespect of women
     B. Radical feminism—the secular glorification of women
     C. Unbridled hedonism—the freedom of sexual expression

II.   The Truth about Gender Equality (Gen 1:16–27)
     A. Both male and female are equal in value, dignity, and worth (vv. 26–27).
     B. Both male and female Christians are equally redeemed and are equally heirs of God's grace (cf. Gal 3:28).

III. The Truth about Gender Differences (Genesis 2)
     A. The reality of gender distinctions
          1. Every human being has been created by God either a male or a female—it is either/or, not both/and (1:27)
          2. Every human being has been created by God to be heterosexual in the expression of their sexuality (1:28; cf. Heb 13:4)
          3. BOTTOM LINE: Same-sex relationships are an abomination to God, the creator of male and female (Lev 18:22–24; 20:13; Rom 1:24–32).
     B. The non-reversible realities of gender differences (Genesis 2)
          1. We men were created first because God intended that we be the leaders (cf. 1 Tim 2:13–14).
          2. We men were created first because God intended that we be the protectors and providers (Gen 2:15).
          3. We men are commanded by God to leave and cleave because God holds us personally responsible as head of our family (2:24).
          4. The woman was created from man's side because God intended that she be her husband's encourager and completer (2:18–25).

Name and Subject Index

Scripture Index

CPSIA information can be obtained
at www.ICGtesting.com
Printed in the USA
LVOW12s0429021116
511081LV00001B/3/P